Twayne's United States Authors Series

Sylvia E. Bowman, *Editor*

INDIANA UNIVERSITY

John Jay Chapman

JOHN JAY CHAPMAN

by **MELVIN H. BERNSTEIN**
Alfred University

 70

Twayne Publishers, Inc.   ::   New York

BECAUSE OF
SARAH AND BEN, ESSIE AND HARRY
FOR
MAE AND HARRIET

Preface

THE MOST PRECIOUS COMMODITY in human history is mind; the most delightful, art. John Jay Chapman was an instance of both. Still, he is known to too few teachers, students, and general readers of American writing. The fact that Harvey Swados omits Chapman from his recent *Years of Conscience* (1962) is much to the point.

The purpose of this study is to trace the origins, growth, and significance of Chapman's ideas. Some of his ideas are clearly identified as long-abiding family interests. Other ideas emerge from the exciting influence of books on a man who loved them. Still other ideas were weapons Chapman used against his times. During his lifetime he stirred controversy, thought, and action. His advice is not obsolete.

In this interpretation, his books are discussed as if Chapman turned his attention mechanically first to politics, then to education, and finally to literature. On the contrary, Chapman's life had a remarkable unity; his thought was intricately organic; and his interests were persistently various. It is no evasion of precision to say that Chapman was in the best sense an eclectic thinker. No one label identifies him. He constantly dignified what he examined by showing in it the indivisible connection between the profane and the sacred. He always left some connection undiagrammed and unidentified, suggesting thereby the ongoing mystery of the search and the attractiveness of the human adventure itself. This is certainly one of his primary charms. It is Chapman the person and the man of his times, poet and dramatist, memoir writer and essayist, literary critic, ethicist and humanist, American and citizen of the world—it is this Chapman who is herein unraveled and, it is hoped, put together again.

Acknowledgments

I wish to acknowledge with thanks the help of the following: Alfred University for a modest abatement of my teaching responsibilities while preparing the manuscript; Alfred University Research Foundation for twice helping me with subsidies to pursue my Chapman research; the many courtesies of the Herrick Memorial Library of Alfred University, the Library of Congress, Swarthmore Library, Princeton Library. and Houghton Library, Harvard University.

My thanks go to Mr. Arthur Deutsch for lending me a rare copy of the *Madison House News*. I am richly indebted to Mr. Chanler A. Chapman, executor of the Chapman papers, and to his wife, Helen, for permission to quote Chapman material; for time spent with me and my correspondence; and for their chastening editorial comments. Professor Sylvia Bowman's editorial advice is incorporated gratefully in the text. The sharp eyes of Mrs. Richard Pearce, who prepared the manuscript for press, saved me frequently from unbecoming carelessness.

Contents

Chronology

1862   John Jay Chapman born on March 2 in New York City.

1876   Entered St. Paul's School, Concord, New Hampshire.

1877   Illness forced him to leave school.

1877-   Privately tutored for college.
1880

1880   Entered Harvard.

1884-   Toured Europe. Visited Spencer, Tennyson, Henry
1885   James, Stevenson.

1885   Entered Harvard Law School.

1887   Burned his left hand in self-punishment for his jealous attack on Percival Lowell, who—Chapman mistakenly fancied—was interested in Minna Timmins. Went to Europe that summer.

1888   Admitted to the New York Bar.

1889   Married Minna Timmins.

1890-   Period of Chapman's active political agitation.
1901

1890   Birth of son, Victor Emmanuel. "Fourth Canto of the *Inferno*," published in the *Atlantic Monthly* in November.

1892   *The Two Philosophers*, a comedy on a Harvard faculty incident, published.

1893   Birth of second son, John Jay Chapman, Jr.

1895   "Michael Angelo's Sonnets," published in *Bachelor of Arts* in June.

1896   Birth of third son, Conrad. "The Young Shakespeare: A Study of Romeo," published in the *Atlantic Monthly* in November. "Browning," published in *Bachelor of Arts* in November and December.

1897   Death of Minna Timmins Chapman a month after the birth of Conrad. "Emerson Sixty Years After," published in the *Atlantic Monthly* in January, February. "Walt Whitman," published in the *Chap-Book* in July.

1897- Edited and published *The Political Nursery,* a private
1901   monthly periodical originally intended to deal with municipal political issues in New York City but later becoming more miscellaneous in content.

1898   Married Elizabeth Chanler. *Emerson and Other Essays* and *Causes and Consequences* published.

1899   Six months in Europe.

1900   *Practical Agitation* published. Awarded an honorary degree of Doctor of Letters by Hobart College, Geneva, New York.

1901   Illness cut off his political activity and required a ten-year period of convalescence. Birth of son, Chanler.

1902- Trip to Europe.
1903

1903   Son, John Jay, drowned in Austria.

1906- Wrote plays, many of them for children.
1911

1907- Trip to Europe.
1908

1908   Published three volumes of plays for children, a total of six slender plays.

1910   *Learning and Other Essays* published. *The Treason and Death of Benedict Arnold: A Play for a Greek Theatre* published.

1911   Trip to Italy and North Africa.

1912   Read Phi Beta Kappa poem at Harvard. Held a memorial service for a Negro lynched in Coatesville, Pennsylvania, in 1911.

1913   Brother, Henry, died. *William Lloyd Garrison* published.

1914   In Europe when World War I started. *Deutschland über Alles; or Germany Speaks* and *Homeric Scenes* published.

1915   *Greek Genius and Other Essays, Memories and Milestones,* and *Notes on Religion* published.

1916   Awarded an honorary degree of Doctor of Letters by Yale. Son, Victor, a member of the Escadrille Lafayette, killed in action. Two volumes of seven plays for children published.

1917   Edited and wrote a memoir for *Victor Chapman's Letters from France.*

1918-   Wrote miscellaneous essays for *Vanity Fair.*
1920

1919   Made a trip to Europe. *Songs and Poems* published.

1921   Chapman's mother died.

1922   *A Glance Toward Shakespeare* published.

1924   *Letters and Religion* published.

1925   Trip to Europe. Resurgence of pamphlet activity on controversial subjects such as Roman Catholic and anti-Semitic prejudice, immigration, Prohibition, and education in America.

1927   *Dante* published.

1928   *Two Greek Plays* published.

1929   *Antigone* published.

1930   Made his last trip to Europe.

1931   *Lucian, Plato and Greek Morals* published. Lectured at Columbia University on higher education.

1932   Worked on his unpublished autobiography, *Retrospections,* and on critical essays on Goethe and Shakespeare.

1933   Died, Vassar Hospital, Poughkeepsie, New York, on November 4.

John Jay Chapman

CHAPTER 1

The Jay-Chapman Ancestry

JOHN JAY CHAPMAN, born during the administration of Abraham Lincoln, died in the administration of Franklin D. Roosevelt. During his active life (1862-1933) he published twenty-five books on various subjects; almost as many pamphlets and privately printed polemics; and numerous poems, never fully collected, in periodicals. He was a prolific and delightful letter writer. The river of his mind emptied naturally into the sea of printer's ink. The body of his writings is a rich example of the continuity in American thought and a small compendium of the heritage of western culture. Somewhat self-consciously, he was what Emerson had challengingly invoked—an American Scholar.

John Jay Chapman was born in a brownstone house a short walk from Washington Square in New York City. He had an older brother, Henry, and was to have two younger sisters, Eleanor and Beatrix; but their influence was to be considerably less than the examples of his father and mother and the achievement of his ancestors.

His father, Henry Grafton Chapman (1833-83), resembled a Henry James capitalist whose nineteenth-century habitat was Washington Square. Born in Boston, a student in the Boston Latin School, a sometime student at Heidelberg, an officer on a merchant ship to China, a founder of the Knickerbocker Club, and president in 1873 of the New York Stock Exchange, Henry Chapman impressed his son as a witty man who talked little, who read devotedly in Shakespeare, who was deeply principled, who was granitic in his chastity, and who left the upbringing of his children to his wife.

Eleanor Jay Chapman exercised her parental responsibility with indulgence and imagination. A well-adjusted matron who might have appeared in the novels of Edith Wharton, she supervised the education of her children; read German, French, and English books; was comfortably at home in Europe during her frequent trips there; and impressed her son John as the image of an old countess of the Continental variety. Both his parents subscribed in theory and in practice to the Chapman family motto engraved on Henry Chapman's ring: *crescit sub pondere virtus*. For all the Jays and the Chapmans in the past, manliness had grown and prospered under the pressure of private adversity and public oppression. In his own life, Chapman was time and again to test the meaning of the motto.

To rehearse briefly the histories of the Jay and the Chapman families is to understand not only how heredity and environment contributed decisively to the development of the mind of John Jay Chapman but also how it came about that he was drawn to certain subjects, was held by them, and had to unburden himself in newspaper, essay, poem, and book. How does it come about that a man who is neither biographer nor historian writes in 1913 a sustained interpretation of William Lloyd Garrison? How does it come about that a translator of Michelangelo's sonnets and of Homer writes on the mystery and charm of the Bible? The answers are found not only in the epochs that might need the reinterpretation—for Chapman's writing has a distinctly public tone—but also in Chapman's identification with his family's motto, history, and tradition of public service to America.

First, the Jay family. Auguste Jay, a militant Huguenot, took up residence in England after the revocation of the Edict of Nantes (1685). His brother, Isaac, died from wounds fighting the Papists at the bloody battle of the Boyne in 1690. Auguste's son, Peter Jay, came to America, married into the Van Cortlandt family, and had eight children, one of whom was John Jay.

John Jay (1745-1829), whose house is even now being restored as a national memorial, was a book buyer and a book lover; a boundary fixer; president of the Continental Congress, Chief Justice of New York, minister to Spain, Chief Justice of the United States, and twice governor of New York; and in retirement president of the Westchester Bible Society and the American Bible Society; an indefatigable writer; organizer of the New York Society for Promoting the Manumission of Slaves; and a lifelong encourager of educational institutions and activities. Although bookish and pious, he moved militantly in public issues, arousing intense public reaction: he was vilified on Boston walls, his figure was carried in dung carts and hung and burnt in effigy. His older brother, Sir James Jay (1732-1815), a physician, was a financier of the American Revolution and a collector of philanthropies for the educational benefit of King's College (Columbia University).

John Jay's two sons carried on the family concern for the public welfare. Peter Augustus Jay (1776-1843) was a successful lawyer, a trustee of Columbia College, a prominent officer of the Episcopal Church, and a president of the New York State Historical Association. William Jay (1789-1858), a judge for twenty-five years, contributed to the first number of the abolitionist *Emancipator;* and, as a pamphleteer and president of the American Peace Society, he made arbitration of international disputes a lifetime cause. A caustic gentleman with an exceedingly sharp pen, William Jay's constitutional arguments against slavery and his demand for immediate, not gradual, emancipation gave example and enthusiasm to his son, John Jay (1817-94), who—while still an undergraduate at Columbia University—was manager of the New York Young Man's Anti-Slavery Society and later, as a lawyer, defended runaway slaves in court.

John Jay created controversy when he urged the admission of a Negro church into the Protestant Episcopal Convention. Later, he became minister to Austria and vice-president of the Civil Service Reform Association of the State of New York. A friend of his observed that this Victorian gentleman—at once reformer, patriot, and ardent Christian whose main interests were antislavery, religion, politics and education—was a tireless writer and vigilant exhorter whose words were as sharp as files. His family's traditional Huguenot hostility to Roman Catholic parochialism erupted in him: he made speeches, wrote pamphlets, and published them at his own expense to forward his view that sectarian education was a deterrent to the proper and necessary American educational ideal. At the age of thirty-four our John Jay Chapman could write to his mother that his grandfather's name and the family tradition were controlling ideas with him ever since he could remember. The evidence for this introspective accuracy is the bibliography of John Jay Chapman. The Jay inheritance in Chapman's life was ineradicable, unmistakable, and potent.

The Chapman side of the family added to John Jay Chapman's inheritance their Puritan dedication, Unitarian conscience, the practice of agitation, and a small shelf of passionate books. His grandmother, Maria Weston (1806-85), of Pilgrim descent, had married Henry Grafton Chapman who had seceded from the Unitarian Church because it was too lethargic in fighting slavery. Mrs. Chapman became the sponsor of the Boston Female Anti-Slavery Society and an international figure known for her hymns, her journalism, her biography of Harriet Martineau, and especially for her flair for dramatizing, publicizing, and agitating the slavery question, at home and abroad. She actively enlisted the support of James Russell Lowell, Victor Hugo, and Harriet Martineau in her cause. She personally protected William Lloyd Garrison. She linked the spirit of Wat Tyler and George Washington to the editorials of the *Liberator*.

Her analytical writings clearly identified the collusive strands of conservative, clerical, financial, and political power which webbed the hypocritical opposition to human freedom, giving what Owen Wister called "a moral squint" to America. Her cause, she was sure, was just; and she could cite the Bible and instances of Nemesis in secular history to clinch the exposition. The test of her times, as she saw it, was how men responded to the question, "Do you love freedom?" She

moralized politics, demanded life according to principle and not subject to mercenary expediencies, named names, and illustrated in her tireless activities that evil was not a cause but a defect. Defects could be corrected. One read and one wrote. One thought and one spoke. One organized and one agitated. Her reform principles had the directness of the self-evident truths taught to children in the nursery.

Both the Jays and the Chapmans had a rich sense of history as it persisted into their own times. Their sense of past and present led them to link their healthy private consciences with the destiny of the America they loved and wished to morally aggrandize. The very name—John Jay Chapman—he wrote in his books, on his papers, in his school books, and at the bottom of his letters made the Jay-Chapman inheritance of service and achievement a constant companion to his thinking, doing, and writing. That it was an ambiguous burden to Chapman appears over and over again in his plays for children—the plays of his most troubled years. In them themes of aristocracy, succession of leadership, crusading, and *noblesse oblige* recur with insistent and revealing persistence.

CHAPTER 2

The Making of the Critic

THE CHILDHOOD of John Jay Chapman was rich in the
memories of the public figures of his ancestry. He was
born during the Civil War, and antislavery had been the
daily conversation of and a messianic passion of his grandparents in whom religion and politics, education and agitation,
books and people, and the Cross and Blindfolded Justice
mingled in a purposeful welter and *Weltanschauung*. There
were the comings and goings of summer vacations on Staten
Island and at Narragansett Pier; the journeys to Grandmother
Chapman's house in Weymouth, Massachusetts; and the visits
to Grandfather Jay's farm in Bedford, New York, not far from
the Hudson. In these history-marked homes were the im-
pressive memorabilia of the past—portraits by Stuart and
Trumbull, marble busts, and books, books, and books. Education and self-cultivation were as normal as breathing. His
mother all her life read in several languages; his father read
regularly in Shakespeare; his brother Henry was an adept
learner in languages and literature. At fourteen Chapman followed his brother Henry to St. Paul's School in Concord,
New Hampshire.

His less than two-year stay at St. Paul's School was a critical
experience for Chapman, both when it happened and in his
own retrospective judgment almost sixty years later. An introspective child who was no longer under the indulgent eye
of his understanding mother and a physically awkward
adolescent who was oppressed by the rigorous chapel and
hymn-singing of the school under the unremitting eyes of the
headmaster Dr. Henry A. Coit, Chapman became physically

ill and mentally distraught. He was taken from school and for four years thereafter was privately tutored for college. In addition, during this handful of years, his experiences with books, music, and the stage marked his artistic sensibilities fathoms-deep. He wandered into city bookshops, heard Anton Rubenstein and Fritz Kreisler play, watched Edwin Booth and James Hackett in Shakespeare, purchased an Aldine Lucian, read steadily in Shakespeare, and repressed a natural inclination toward the Romantic poets in favor of Pope and the constraints of neo-Classicism. His lifelong friendship with Owen Wister, who genuinely understood his impulsive friend, dates from this period.

At Harvard College (1880-84) Chapman's Washington Square angularities were smoothed by the substantial culture machine of the college, the convivial Cambridge student life, and the ambient, hierarchical social life of Boston. His teachers marked for life his intellectual enthusiasms and prejudices. In his room he ardently practiced the violin, trying to wrest from it the inexpressible secret of the universe. (His avid desire to express in music the tantalizingly inexpressible in himself lasted to the words he spoke just before he died: "I want to play on the open strings.") Social Boston offered dinner parties, pretty girls, famous names of vintage families, memorable *bon mots*, and the industrious hum of literary salons designed to encourage good conversation and to reinforce the locally accepted notion that Massachusetts was not only a place but also a civilization. Chapman maintained an excited, admiring, insider-outsider attitude toward Boston and its bewildering variety of genteel, social, and literary Brahmins. In his later essay on Emerson and particularly in his effervescent letters, he enjoyed isolating and defining the peculiar but less-than-sovereign treasure that had been Boston.

The college years were ones of reading in the classics and of pitting the secular philosophers against the family-ingrained religious definitions of his young-man's universe. Darwinism and Spencerianism seriously shook his faith. He spent many hours hard at work on essays for Harvard's magazines, literary societies, and clubs. And he was writing poetry of a revealing auto-didactic kind. M. A. DeWolfe Howe, Chapman's first biographer, cites a poem probably from the period 1883-85 which intimates the turmoil of an outwardly debonair young man who secretly senses the steps of the Hound of Heaven:

> O God, when the heart is warmest,
> And the head is clearest,
>   Give me to act—
> Turn the purposes Thou formest
>   Into fact.[1]

The stirrings of creativity in music, in poetry, in lively letters, in intense sessions with the poetry of Robert Browning and the essays of Emerson, in the excitements of healthy man-flesh (but unassuaged by love affairs), in evenings at the theater and concert hall, in the pleasure of making his correspondents rise to the bait of his witty and uninhibited opinions on everything and everyone who got caught in his ink—these should have unerringly directed Chapman to his career of writer, of critic. Instead, at the back of his mind were "gloomy forebodings awakened by prospective Law . . . a world that is neither science nor poetry, nor social life nor religion, though it impinges upon them all, and is pieced out of them all."[2] He received a graduation gift of a fifteen-month European tour during which he visited Spencer, Tennyson, the Thackeray family, Henry James, Robert Louis Stevenson, and a relative who was a German ambassador. He began his study of Italian with Dante and a pocket dictionary. He visited Russia. Returning to drab America, Chapman matriculated into the Harvard Law School.

Chapman worked hard in law school, but his unfocused desires were strongly against his easy success. Ambivalence took its toll. He became nervous about his eyes, hired readers to read to him, and persevered. He enjoyed the friendship of Judge Oliver Wendell Holmes; the fraternal life of his fellow students; the conviviality of Beacon Street parties; mountain resorts; and the shared experiences of six years' living in and around the Hub of the Universe. Besides, he was with great unconsciousness and with almost incredible naïveté falling in love.

He had met Minna Timmins, an Italian-American, who was gay, intense, religious, beautiful, and especially adept in Italian. Together they read Dante. Jealous and mistaken about the attentions of Percival Lowell to Minna, Chapman impulsively thrashed Lowell, returned to his room, held his left hand in the hearthfire and burned it so severely it had to be amputated.[3] In this dramatic way was Chapman's love for Minna published. Minna's family reluctantly recognized the claim of Chapman's love but prescribed a separation for a year. Minna went west; Chapman recovered slowly, went to Europe that summer, returned to read law in a relative's office, and was admitted to the bar.

These had been excruciatingly unhappy years for Chapman. He had persisted in the study of law for which he had the slenderest aspirations. He had discovered the pathological depths of his emotional nature. He had been separated, except for a letter-writing intimacy, from Minna. He had lost a hand, gained a profession, and won a wife whom he married in 1889. He was apparently determined to make his way in New York City public life. His ambition to be a writer was forcibly kept down. "Better cast a vote than write a book," he wrote to his affianced in 1884.[4] The image of his family as public leaders, as good bourgeois, controlled his outward ambition. After all, a man had to support his wife, and literature was certainly not the way to do so.

Some aspects of law attracted him. Compared with other young lawyers, he wrote an excellent brief. But writing briefs bored him. He craved to be a man of action; he would have loved to be a trial lawyer, but his law firm held him down. He drifted away from law and into politics. He joined the City Reform Club, which had been started in 1882 by Theodore Roosevelt, among others. To end ballot stuffing, repeating, and strong-arm methods, he watched the polls and tried to get honest election laws enforced. Dissatisfied with the machine politics of both Tammany Hall and the Republicans, he went independent with the Good Government Clubs (he was president of one unit), and later he tried to achieve his goals in fusion party politics.

The decade 1890-1900 was a vigorous and hectic period in his life. He enjoyed his marriage, and three sons were born. He worked indefatigably in the melting pot of a New York City teeming with exploited immigrants, fecund in corruption, but rich in a way that distinguished America from Europe at the end of the nineteenth century: Americans were decidedly optimistic. America was perfectible. Vice was a remediable defect. America was the future. Reformers looked into the promised land of the twentieth century with confidence. Chapman could see like Moses; but he would also act like Joshua: "My line of politics is war—war—war—with an ideal of absolute good humor and self-control."[5]

All of the excitement of being and doing during this decade of Chapman's life is caught in the first three books he published and in the oversize pages of a private periodical he wrote, edited, and published. One of the books, *Emerson and Other Essays* was primarily literary and will be noticed later; the other two books, *Causes and Consequences* (1898) and *Practical Agitation* (1900) were coherent analyses of his miscellaneous experiences of the decade, many of them freshly recorded in the thirty-six issues of *The Political Nursery* (1897-1901). The *Nursery* mirrors the life and times of Chapman; and, when examined in detail (no formal analysis of it has been printed), prefigures precisely the causes, passions, insights, values, literary art, and educative intentions of Chapman's cultural criticism. It started in high fun and ended in personal disaster. He nailed his challenging theses on the walls of the New York City Chamber of Commerce. The struggle ensued, complete with civil war in Chapman's mind. It took him ten years to recover from the effort.

CHAPTER 3

The Mirror of Politics

THE JAYS no less than the Chapmans had taken to journalism with energy and deftness to advance their commonwealth causes. John Jay had made his contributions to the *Federalist* papers; Maria Chapman had edited the *Non-Resistant*, the *Liberator*, and most of the fifteen issues of the *Liberty Bell*.[1] More recently as an example to emulate, Chapman's brother Henry had been publishing a magazine, *Bachelor of Arts* (1895-98). Its essays are a list of the concerns of the day and his family's causes: internationalism, religion, capitalistic individualism, science free from ecclesiastical dogmas, democracy and law in political reform, and conscience as the pragmatic sanction in civic affairs. The *Bachelor*, because of its failure to gain wide circulation, folded. But before it ended, Chapman had started his own periodical.

I The Political Nursery

The Political Nursery is in appearance such a helter-skelter journal that it easily frightens off investigators or amuses its casual readers into indolent toleration and easy forgetting. It ran from March, 1897, to January, 1901, for a total of thirty-six issues, including two supplements. Printed on different sizes of paper, it averaged four pages per issue, and sold for ten cents a copy. The paper carried a motto: "Let break what must break, / We shall soon see the way." The name of the magazine may go back to the anonymous periodical *The Political Nursery for the Year Eighteen Hundred Two*, published in Norwich, Connecticut, or the title may be ascribed simply to Chapman's inspiration and bias. Chapman asserted with a wise ingenuousness that the simple nursery truths were those of morality and good conduct. The mast of all issues announced his intention: "The object of THE NURSERY is to tell the truth. There is no publication at present which seems to cover this exact field. Truth is the best seen by the light of example, hence THE NURSERY does not shun personalities, when they are in point."

This statement was Chapman's declaration of war against the New York *Times, Herald, Sun, Post,* and the *Nation.* Contributors named Uncle Tom, Aunt Serena, Georgie, Fido, Nursey, Fluff, and Susy signed their names to the satirical nursery lessons. Elementary rate × time = distance arithmetic problems were offered: "If Judge Barrett and Richard Croker travelled South on the same train, what relation, if any, has the fact to the proposed union of dishonest Tammany and Honest National Democracy . . . this fall?" (March, 1897, 4).

The *Nursery* started off in the pop-gun and firework style of Washington Irving's irreverent treatment of New York's great names. In 1897 Chapman believed that humor, "the ratsbane for hypocrites," was better than denunciation. He used almost every rhetorical device and satirical form to wound his brand of political subversive—the moral cripple. His targets were not primarily the politicians but his fellow clubmen and the "dishonest respectables" who collaborated with them. He pointed to 150 different public issues in editorials exploiting saucy query, gay epigram, telling quotation, funny dialogue, legalistic cross-examination, open letter, satirical drama, apt parody of Old Testament style, journalistic poems (23), judicious book reviews (10), finally lapsing into serious philosophical essays.

Chapman may have started out merely to sabotage the machine politics of New York City, but in time he extended himself to comment on the Boer War, the Dreyfus Case, the function of a university, the intrinsically evil propaganda of Kipling, and the paradoxical victory of non-resistance. In the beginning he anticipated the exposures of Lincoln Steffens and the fiction of Upton Sinclair, Ernest Poole, and Frank Norris; and his prose supplements the photographs of Jacob Riis's compassionate camera. Unlike Henry James's John Marcher, Chapman early recognized the Beast in the Jungle; but, instead of waiting, he sprang. What he recognized was, in a word, degeneration, the evil he was sensitized to by his acute observation and by his reading, certainly, of Emerson and, perhaps, of Max Nordau.

His politics were a mixture of Aristotle and the Bible. Since right doing was dependent upon right thinking, where had politicians, lobbyists, machine members, corrupt senators, governors, newspaper editors, and bribed judges gone wrong? They had lost the inspiration of elementary nursery truths. They had put their energies to wrong uses for the wrong ends. "The canker of the times is moral cowardice"—especially of "the Better Element," whose insincerity and hypocrisy made them into Lord Chesterfields, not gentlemen. More than being traitors to their responsible class, the clubmen had betrayed democracy. The shame of New York City was attributable to particular men; the disgrace of America was the weakness that sapped her democracy—America, the potential instructor of still feudal Europe. The bribed decision, the predetermined primary, and the closed lips of the timid electorate had ominous international significance. Chapman, like Walt Whitman, was angry at democratic vistas obscured. "The American-at-home is a whipped animal. . . . His main fear throughout life is that he may be thought eccentric, express an opinion and lose money. . . . If your juries will not save you, your statutes will never do it" (May, 1897, 2).

Heroes, villains, and fence-sitters emerged in the pages of the periodical. Carl Schurz supported Civil Service Reform: he was a hero—one of the most interesting figures on the Continent of North America, Chapman said. When Theodore Roosevelt made deals in the back room, he worshiped neither God nor Mammon but the Deity known as "The Boys." He was a villain. The fence-sitters whom Chapman tried to convert to action, the moral mugwumps, say the Citizens Union, the City Club, and the unintimidated but disconsolate Independent Voter—at these he aimed his exasperated encouragement. Of a certain two hundred "heavy respectables," that is, two hundred substantial citizens who in signing a public petition hoped muddleheadedly for reform, Chapman parodied:

> Half a deal, half a deal, half a deal onward,
>   Into real politics,
>   Into a dreadful mix
> Rode the two hundred. . . .
>
> Mammon to right of them
> Mammon to left of them
> Mammon in front of them
> Bullied and thundered.
>   (Midsummer, 1897, 4)

With Byron's anger at cant, and in the manner of Carlyle's Herr Diogenes Teufelsdrockh, Chapman urged his peer group to take up the responsibility of government according to principle:

> Do you not think, you Mr. Church Deacon Bank-President, you Mr. Senior Warden Gas-President, you, Mr. Franchise Grabber Charity-Patron, you, the Rev. Politic Polyglot, you, Dr. Millionairist Physic, you, Lawyer Corporation-Fee-Taker, you, Architect Smug-Face, you, Merchant Food Adulterator, you Manufacturer Short Roll, you, Gentleman Do Nothing, and all you other innumerables who go to make up the upper ten, the Heavy Respectables, the persons who have influence in the community because of their money, or their clothes, or their social position, or their God-Knows-What, possibly ancestors' swindling, certainly not because of righteous thinking or righteous dealing, do you not think that you had better stop this prating about your own desire to vote according to the dictates of what you are pleased to call your conscience, and about your fear that other persons will not vote according to theirs? Do you not think that you had better begin to ask whether you are not a humbug? (Midsummer, 1897, 3-4).

[32]

When Joseph H. Choate and Elihu Root (heavy respectables) either by omission or commission failed in Chapman's estimation to support reform, they had made a direct assault on the community, an undisguised attack upon American liberties, and they were traitors to the Republic. Chapman always had the large view in mind: he saw infinity in a grain of sand.

Alas, the poor citizens. They were between the devil (Tammany or the Republican machine) and the deep sea of business corporation tyranny. When they rode on the city's electric trolley cars, they risked their lives. Not safety but money in unholy alliance with political eyeblinking and the suppression of accident reports by newspapers ruled the negligent operation of the transit system. The people, Chapman wrote, were like King Lear who, in his generous madness, had given up everything. It followed that if they listened to truth-telling Fool Chapman, they could recover from their madness if they tried. The remedy was: "Cast your vote for a principle that will survive the election" (September-October, 1900, 6). To Chapman, ideas were weapons with which to win elections.

In the early years of the *Nursery,* Chapman had huge reservoirs of good humor even though he found scant hope anywhere, but rather numerous organic filaments of corruption and degradation. The Populists and Socialists failed to enlist his support because they were too self-interested in their doctrinaire economic view of the country's good; man did not live by bread alone. Ring rule and corporation rule, the larger issue, applied to Washington as it did to New York City. Newspapers failed their readers because they were apologists for incompetency in public office. Financiers and corruptors mingled socially at a musicale in Perry Belmont's home in New York and in the cloak rooms of Congress. The new Waldorf Astoria Hotel was a beguiling monument to *la dolce vita,* not to the good life. Theodore Roosevelt's cant of manifest destiny was as fraught with self-destruction as the actual, scandalous mismanagement of the services of supply to the soldiers of the Spanish-American War. American politics, Chapman insisted, was potentially more than an extension of the blunders of English politics. America must reject Kipling as a class poet of race prejudice, thereby instructing England (even as Alexis De Tocqueville and W. E. H. Lecky had suggested) in the difference between a Cecil Rhodes and a David Livingstone (April, 1899, 9). As the Boer War progressed, Chapman became more bitter about the crude goals of English imperialism: "All that glitters in the Transvaal is—just the gold" (January, 1900, 2). Man could not live by gold alone.

He linked the Dreyfus Case with the lynch law of England in Africa, of America in the Philippines, and, significantly, of America at home. He dourly commented: "Nine hundred cases of lynching in three years in the Southern States is a good record" (January, 1900, 3). The American task was not to ape England, for our past had directed us otherwise. To defect from the obvious path of our history (a manifest moral destiny decisively different from Theodore Roosevelt's and the image projected by the yellow press of the era) was to destroy our symbolic value to and for the future. He saw America rather in the image of the good bourgeois he himself was: America was "like a man who has inherited great wealth, we have no excuse for being mean," brutalizing ourselves, filling our speech and our posture with words and attitudes of brag, making ourselves more vulnerable to the destructive passions of war (May, 1900, 4).

The politics of his native city had grown to include the politics of his country, of England, of France, and, indeed, of the world. The corrupt politician merged in his Abolition-haunted mind with the lyncher of Negroes. Chapman's conscience had caught the cosmos in which justice and love, the head and the heart, were locked in a gigantic, painful embrace; and its pain Chapman felt in the marrow of his bones. That was the way virtue increased. Before he succumbed to his mauling, he published two extended analyses—diagnosis and prognosis—of the malady of modern life. They were *Causes and Consequences* and *Practical Agitation*.

II Causes and Consequences

Ruin, Shakespeare confessed in a sonnet, taught him to ruminate. The pain of losing an election led Chapman to write the ruminative *Causes and Consequences,* a brief conduct book based not on manners but on morals. The elementary definition of Chapman's man asserted that, although man was both selfish and unselfish, it made a significant difference to say which he was primarily. Chapman insisted that man was primarily unselfish but was being morally distorted by the pressures of life around him to behave selfishly. Wherever Chapman looked, whether at society, education, democracy, or government (his four chapter headings), he searched for the coil spring of conduct and growth which, unfortunately, had been cramped—but only temporarily he optimistically hoped—by the selfish ethos of commercialism.

Searching out the cause, he found a clue in American history, particularly in the Civil War. Itself a consequence, it was also a cause of other things. The Civil War had been crucial economically for America. Government based not on altruistic principle but on money was the post-bellum native development that qualified every aspect of American life in the succeeding forty years. Agriculture had yielded to finance capitalism; the farm had yielded to the city; de Crevecoeur's resilient American had declined into De Tocqueville's bland American; and the depersonalization of organic, democratic, educative, and social life in America had established itself.

The two major symbols of this traumatic change were the city and the railroad. When a railroad was put through an American city, at that moment the urban (railroad) civilization had its inception. The big-business civilization founded on the morality of money was the cause; the consequences were inevitable. The political machine, the tyrannical "boss," favors, bribery, malfeasance, equivocation, patronage, simony, the legal immunity of the rich and the powerful, the disregard of the citizen, the pooh-poohing of reform as visionary, social prejudices, oligarchic conservatism, civic apathy—all were destructive of democracy. The sophistry of commerce in America's Gilded Age had made the worst the better cause: "The sudden creation of wealth in the United States has been too much for our people. We are personally dishonest. . . . Out of this comes the popular philosophy, the social life, the architecture, the letters, the temper of the age; all tinged with the passion."[2] Just as the politico-economics of slavery as represented by Beacon Street had defined American life before the Civil War, so commerce was inhibiting and disfiguring America about to enter the twentieth century. The present had turned uniform, and the lesson of the American past was neglected.

Chapman's remedy was individualism reconsidered: "Everything depends as completely on personal intercourse as it did in Athens. The real struggle comes between two men across a table, my force against your force."[3] It was, then, a secularized religious ideal of service he recommended to the insurgent individual, to the resurgent American individual whose history had promised him active, moral, decision-making participation in his self-government. American democracy was not whole-hog self-advancement: "the reverse is true. The merit lies in the assumption imposed upon every man that he shall serve his fellow man."[4] The guerilla warfare waged against hardships that Chapman participated in and witnessed (Jane Addams, Edward Bellamy, Christian Endeavorers, Salvation Army, Jewish philanthropy, Christian missions, private humanitarianism in settlement projects) was the post-war Underground Railroad—a better railroad, obviously—of the movement to freedom in men of conscience and rectitude. To the question, "What's in it for me?" the answer was, "Nothing except life according to principle." Man the reformer asked nothing for himself; his task was the education of other people. The individual's personal behavior was an unconscious educational force to many. Good behavior was contagious by example. Independence had the power to create a community; and from many, America's motto rightly suggested, came one.

Causes and Consequences received considerable critical notice. Its idealism, optimism, and literary gracefulness were all praised. It reportedly circulated in a paperback edition. But however long it was in moralism, it was short in the sagacities of practical, American, party politics. It was almost, the critics noticed, too Emersonian. It encouraged too much independence, too much separatism. Chapman would agree; in fact, he did agree. It did encourage independence but not separatism. He went his own Emersonian way in his next book, *Practical Agitation,* his last book devoted solely to political reform.

III Practical Agitation

The more Chapman reflected on the high and low jinks of elections, the fallow period between elections, the confusing behavior of the electorate (before and after opinion polls), and the behavior of the journals of news, opinion, and literature, the more he was convinced that all of them were interconnected (as, indeed, they are) and that all suffered from a signal defect. "Which national party stands for an idea today?" he asked.[5] Because neither did, a third party could. And what did a third party effect? Even if it did not obtain election victory, at least it established the force of insult, the example of popular rebellion, and the influence of its thoughtful dissent.

A third party was the refuge of the independent, of the American individual steam-rollered by anonymous machine parties, conformist machine loyalties, and perverse machine superstitions which knew no morality. The abandoned secret of politics was morality, and the voter must be offered a moral ideal for which to vote. This was the idea so lacking in both major American parties. After all, government went on night and day and the citizen of integrity had the option of agitating for moral government between elections. Opinion making was to be encouraged always—at dinner, at a party, on the street, or over a glass of beer. By informed talk, the citizen could constantly challenge the new priestly class of commerce and inaugurate reform. Had not the citizens of Boston and New York spoken out against the old priestly class of slaveholders and slavery defenders? Jesus had been no soft handler of hypocrites. "You must talk facts, you must name names, you must impute motives. You must say what is on your mind."[6] To do so was to distress the conservatism of members of the Union League Club (Chapman's decaying class), to introduce truthtelling into the kept-press of American journalism, and become that mysterious but effective quantity in life—a source and force of personal influence with the celebrated power to crack the "gloomy ice-field, the American civic consciousness."[7] Not the world but the people in it were the source of the degradation of the times. Subject neither to fatalism nor to the determinisms of biology or economics, man was perfectible because his intelligence and will could be stirred by the irrepressible tendencies of unselfish man toward right feeling and right doing.

This moral pragmatism was not very much, it can be said, for a man to learn after ten years of New York political cockfighting. But it was abiding. Chapman steadfastly refused to accept the utilitarian stratagem of compromise that so frequently accompanies political infighting. The two books and the *Nursery* had alienated him from his class, had disenchanted him with law, had fatigued him with day-to-day commitments, and had led him not to Machiavelli but to Tolstoi and to the Old and the New Testament. His impatience with the techniques of political science and emergent sociology had made him declare in a meeting of the American Academy of Political and Social Science in April, 1898, "I am on the side of the revivalist."[8] The *Nation* reviewer was right when he wrote of *Practical Agitation* that it was "the sort of thing we expect to hear in church. . . . Nevertheless, it is true."[9] The wanness of exhortation and the appeal to the old ethics as it applied to the robust materialism and secularism emerging in the twentieth century are here underlined in

Chapman and in the influential *Nation's* comment. The residue of moralism for the Good Old Cause (notice how many parallels Chapman drew between ante- and post-bellum Civil War America) later culminated in his book on the political importance of neglected, almost forgotten William Lloyd Garrison in 1913. It explains in part why Chapman was sure that the history of nineteenth-century America would be rewritten with Garrison at the center.

Chapman, the critic of American civilization, had been tried in the crucible of public events and private vicissitude. The struggle was costly. Unhusbanded political, journalistic, and literary efforts (the last to be noticed in another chapter); the private grief suffered in the death of his first wife (1897); and the compensatory joy in his marriage to Elizabeth Chanler in 1898—all combined to push Chapman to the tenuous limits of his endurance. His failure to organize a third party that would prevent Theodore Roosevelt's successful fight for the governorship of New York finally exhausted him. The clear prophecy of his imminent collapse was revealed in his public diary, the *Nursery*, in the May, 1900, issue, in a poem, "Non-Resistance": Humanity was not moved by argument; he was tired of reiterating that humanity is sick; better to keep quiet and live a life of example.

> Must you be propping others with your crutch?
> Just stand alone and show us how it's done.
> Your plan of walking doesn't matter much
> So long as you apparently get on.
> Just walk alone.

A little more than a year later, he was put to bed in a darkened room from which he did not stir for months. The *Nursery* had made the adult as helpless as an infant. Had he had the spirit to look into the mirror of politics during that winter of 1901 he would have seen reflected in it Truth unimpaired and a bearded, broken, silent man curled up in a child's self-defensive posture.

Recovery was tremulously slow, complete with previsioned

crutches; but it was accompanied with a richness of a mind largely subdued to its more introspective, more artistic imperatives.

IV   *Political Reflections in His Plays*

During the ten years of his recovery he wrote plays for children. Some of them were acted by children in the family at Tarrytown and at the University Settlement in New York City. Plays like *The Lost Prince, King Ithuriel, The Hermits,* and *Christmas in Leipsic* with their wrecked old men in a "brain sick wonderland," children thought dead and restored miraculously to life, good governors who desire love and wicked politicians who desire power, reminiscences of "youth, and love, and hot-head rivalry," exclamations of guilt, self-recriminations about duty neglected, sin, and suicide, pious sentiments about repentance, conversion, and the contentment "that God doth use us towards his ends"—all reflect the troubled mind submitting to the curative purge of art. They are plays difficult to act, spotted with Latin, French, and English archaisms; they are the delicate debris of grief unforgotten, certainly for his drowned son Jay (1903), and the defeat of altruism by the devils of self-seeking politics. Nor is the content much different in a later volume of four plays, *Neptune's Isle* (1911). Adopted children, children sacrificed to appease death, children leading adults to peace and God, Lazarus reborn, a crippled Christian with a crutch—these are the artistic detritus of Chapman's eroded pain. The most sunny of the four plays, the one in which Chapman's sharp observation and delightful humor break through the miasma of his spirit, is *Neptune's Isle.* Chapman's troubled mind of this period was like Mark Twain's after the death of his daughter Susie.

In January, 1908, in Tours, France, Chapman had put the finishing touches to *The Maid's Forgiveness,* a play set in Germany in the 1100's. In strong blank verse marked with Shakespearian prosodic imitation and with overtones of *Hamlet,* Chapman made it rehearse his abiding cares. It is replete with suggestive leads to Richard Hovey's thesis that deep, unresolved father-son-mother tensions were primary and primal causes of Chapman's early neuroticism. In the play the king's mind crumbles from within by a "sin" undisclosed and from without by pressures of a scheming "doctor" hungry for power. The mirrors of his memory reflect distortions; and the life in the castle is similarly distorted until a crucifix, the symbol of "love, pain, and death," is uncovered in a judicial inquiry involving the "dry bones of law," thus unraveling the unhappiness.

The Maid's Forgiveness is a murky window open on Chapman's mind manfully struggling with its desire for self-control in the decade of his temporary debility at the turn of the century. It is rich in allusions to the power of music "that burns in the heart like tears unshed." It is equally clear in its acceptance of patience to deal with obstinate thoughts and of the doctrine of non-resistance. The prince who loses his throne and finds himself says:

> We all are planets,
> Which live within each other's influence,
> Controlled, protected, passing to eclipse,
> Or reappearing in the effulgent sun
> Through the same power, which by our apprehension
> Becomes ourself. And if a man will trust it,
> I give him leave to call it what he will,—
> Love, thought, illusion, destiny, or God.[10]

The Treason and Death of Benedict Arnold (1910) was almost the signal of Chapman's recovery from morbid introspection, tortured self-incrimination for public and private failures, and the literary unimaginativeness that had made his other plays of the period of his healing mind seem the monotonous circling of a crippled Pegasus hitched to the fixed pole that turned an antique millstone. This play was not set in fantasied Germany of the Middle Ages; it looked out upon the Hudson River scenery of his Tarrytown residence. It was not clotted with pseudo-Elizabethan form and rhetoric; it was a creative breakthrough to adapting the scheme of a Greek play with chorus to American history. It was not a story of peasants who were really of noble birth or of lost children who were finally found; it was a story of Oedipus confronting himself, of *ubris* self-discovered, of identity faced. The refining fire of pain allowed Benedict Arnold to acknowledge the abysmal reaches of character and personality. The chorus observes: "All men become something incredible to themselves." One step more allowed Chapman the balm of Gilead: "God forgets not the virtue of those who have failed."

Almost a contradiction to C. B. Todd's *The Real Benedict Arnold* (1903), which had pinned the blame of Arnold's defection on Arnold's second wife, Chapman had Arnold explicitly say that his reason had been deliberate: "All was conceived before I married you." This conversation between husband and wife gave Chapman an opportunity to proclaim the end of his sequestered convalescence and his sensitively felt dependence upon the understanding and love of his own wife: "I will sing a song of woman, and magnify the wife of a man's soul." It was a literary thank-you note for his wife's loving ministrations. The play was acted once with Ben Greet and another time with Walter Hampden playing leading roles; Chapman himself read it to a Harvard audience; it won praise from scholars like Richard Moulton and from teachers like George Baker at Harvard. The Bible and Greek literature together had driven the ten plagues from his mind.

V *His Return to Practical Agitation*

All this while Chapman had been fashioning himself into a literary critic by writing translations of Dante and Michelangelo's sonnets and by publishing interpretive essays on Shakespeare, Browning, Whitman, Stevenson, and Emerson. He confessed that it had been Emerson that had set him free, made him think he was just as good as the next man, and invigorated his own independence, radicalism, and fond-

ness for agitation. After he was well on the way to physical
and intellectual recovery, Chapman addressed himself to a
study of a practical agitator, William Lloyd Garrison, and
published in 1913 a solid and exciting evaluation of his role
in provoking the passion of dissent in a conservative time.
Garrison stood symbolically for the neglected spiritual side
of the American of the nineteenth century. As such, he was
tonic to the twentieth-century America as it was to be described by Reinhold Niebuhr and Walter Lippmann.

Studying the memorabilia of the Garrison period, Chapman
was richly moved, alternately horrified and ennobled, in his
feelings about man at war. He himself had been born during
the beginnings of the Civil War in which his family's most
earnest interests had been implicated. They had been for
constitutional means, for persuasion, for exhortation, and for
the reformation of the slavery question by moral renovation
rather than by force. He was ashamed that his own father paid
to have a man serve in his place in the Union Army. Escape
from the moral judgment of war seemed to him impossible;
it was nemesis. The Civil War was not to Chapman a historical night when all cats were gray; nor had it been so to
his family. Rather, it was mythic in force. It was a regrettable affair, but richly didactic. It had educated America
(and the watching world) to the imperatives of conscience,
the root-and-branch structure of man's altruism, and to the
painful truth that virtue grows under, through, and in spite
of pressure. There is ample evidence from his earliest publica-
tions of his preoccupation with the precepts and morality
of war.

For example, in the *Nursery* he had expressed ambivalent
feelings about the Spanish-American War. Regretting its
start, he had to accept it as fact. He was inexperienced in
observing a nation at war, and what he saw impressed him
in a peculiar light. He noticed the nation no longer distracted
by William Jennings Bryan, Eugene V. Debs, labor struggles,
or sectionalism but united—almost in a religious mood. The
war had taken America's mind off making money—a good

omen. So long as America did not exploit the Filipinos, she was safe in honor. Surely, America was not like the Germany of 1898, a frightening empire fulfilling the organized hatred bred into it by Bismarck.

That Chapman had dived deep into the baffling sources of energy propelling men into the calculated fury of war is reflected in his poem "Lines on the Death of Bismarck," printed in the July, 1898, midsummer supplement of *Nursery*. Chapman later collected a truncated version in *Songs-and Poems* from which the Viking Portable Library *Poets of the English Language*, edited by W. H. Auden and N. H. Pearson, took its copy. Both versions omitted, however, the following forty lines of powerful verse that reveal the perceptiveness of Chapman and his prescient imagination projecting the abysmal reaches of Nazi war-hate:

Organized hatred. Educated men
Live in habitual scorn of intellect,
Hate France, hate England, hate America.
Talk corporals, talk until Napoleon
(—Who never could subdue the mind of France—)
Seems like some harmless passing episode,
Unable to reveal to modern man
What tyranny could compass. Years of this
Will leave a Germany devoid of fire,
Unlettered, unrebellious, impotent,
Nursing the name of German unity
And doing pilgrimage to Bismarck's shrine,
Bismarck the god, who having but one thought,
Wrote it out largely over Germany
But could not stay to read it. Those who can,
Who reap the crop he sowed may count the grains
And every seed a scourge. For on the heart
One or a million, each envenomed throb
Relentlessly records an injury,
While the encrusted nation loses health,
And like a chemical experiment
The crucible gives back its quantities.

The thing this man employed so cleverly
Was poison then, and poison in the end,
And Germany is writhing in its grip.
They paid their liberties and got revenge—
The ancient bargain. But upon a scale
A scope, a consequence, a stretch of time
That made a camp of Europe, and set back
The cultured continent for centuries.
The fear of firearms has dwarfed the French
To gibbering lunatics; and Zola's friends
And all that France can show for commonsense.
Italy's bankrupt, Russia barbarous
Kept so by isolation, and the force,
The only force that can improve the world,
Enlightened public thought in private men,
Is minimized in Europe, till The Powers
Stand over Crete to watch a butchery
And diplomats decide the fate of men.

Like twentieth-century man's futile pursuit of a "clean bomb," Chapman seems to have desired a "clean war." In the meantime, he publicized obvious unsavory aspects of war activity and psychology.

He registered repugnance at rumors of profiteering in the Spanish-American War. He angrily rebuked Theodore Roosevelt for his bellicose temperament and athletic imperialism. Similarly, the force of the British push against the Boers angered him. Bloodshed and commercial interests in the name of jingoism described for him the conflict. There were touches of biblical frenzy in his *Nursery* editorials and poems on the subject. He urged the British to be Pharaoh and let the Boers go; perhaps, if they did, they might be saved from worshiping the Golden Calf (January, 1900, 2). The important thing for America was not to get embroiled in the "dust and ashes of European ambition." The war atrocities in Asia, Africa, and in the Pacific were not without their repercussions in America: he noticed that Americans were baiting Negroes more and more (September-October, 1900, 2).

The Negro in America was very much in his mind while he was writing his biography of Garrison. In 1911 a Negro was lynched in Coatesville, Pennsylvania. On the first anniversary of his death Chapman went to Coatesville and rented a store for a commemorative prayer meeting attended by one or two other persons. In his independent fashion Chapman was penitentially protesting in a deeply reverent sense against the state of the human heart. Widely reprinted in its day, collected as "Coatesville" in *Memories and Milestones,* the speech implicated Everyman in the guilt of vengeful and unapprehended murder. "Whatever life itself is, that thing must be replenished in us. The opposite of hate is love, the opposite of cold is heat; what we need is the love of God and reverence for human nature. . . . For this truth touches all ages and affects every soul in the world," he said.[11] What is indicated here is the quiet, forcefully muted, prophetic-religious intensity below the muffled excitement of the Coatesville speech.

A few years later, during the summer of 1914, the Chapman family were in Germany. They made their way to England with difficulty. The wars that Chapman had escaped by birth and chance, the wars that had energized his family before him, at last came close to him. War fever excited an easily irritated man, not too long ago sick unto death and despairing of balm in Gilead, not merely for himself but for all men. He had a cause again. To it he gave himself, his pen, and for it he was to lose his son Victor.

No sooner back in England, he wrote letters to newspapers urging America to enter the war against Germany, and planned a memorandum on compulsory disarmament (a Jay family enterprise) in which he enlisted the personal support of Lord Balfour, Lord Haldane, Henry Adams, Henry Cabot Lodge, and President Wilson. Without the assurance that the war would culminate in this "emancipation proclamation" ending wars among nations, the educative potentiality of even a victorious war would be lost. His ideas were supported by those of Sir Norman Angell, whose *The Lost Illusion* (1911) Chapman had read and annotated in 1912. He was convinced that Germany's militaristic aggression was a species of unreason. War was the necessary therapy.

He collected Pan-Germanic ideological statements of leading Germans and published them in *Deutschland über Alles, or Germany Speaks* (1914). Germany was pathologically war-minded, Chapman asserted; and he supplied documentary evidence culled from the utterances of representative German military leaders, statesmen, poets, and scholars to prove it. The long habit of German dogmatism and the narrow practice of German educational specialism had constricted the German mind until it was capable of believing in and acting aggressively upon its own delusions. Germany was sick, but defeat in war would cure her. His friend, Owen Wister, in *The Pentecost of Calamity* (1915), echoed Chapman's observations and, similarly, could not abide "moral neutrality" in the matter. Chapman was for war—for moral, educational reasons. Germany's madness had to be put into a strait jacket of defeat, peace, and compulsory disarmament.

As a neutral of French descent on the Jay side of the family, and with Victor signed up in the French Legion, Chapman worked sympathetically for French relief. He wrote a children's tableau-play, *Lafayette*. It was produced in New York in 1915, the proceeds going to the Lafayette Fund Committee. (Émile Legouis, the French scholar, translated it into French, and Richard Harding Davis wrote an epilogue for it.) Chapman still admired England, for it had given his family asylum in the late 1600's. He talked intervention in Washington, D.C. He worried about Victor. Attending church daily during the war helped to alleviate his worry about his other son, Conrad, an ensign on escort duty in the United States Naval Reserve.

At Verdun, Victor, twenty-seven, then a member of the Escadrille Lafayette, was killed, the first American aviator to die in the war. His death was an international matter, exhaustively publicized in the magazines and newspapers of the day. Victor's letters to his family, Chapman felt, were a tribute

to the French religion of humanity. He collected and published them in 1917, at the same time writing a tender,
prefatory memorial of Victor's mother, Chapman's first wife.

When America declared war, Chapman wrote a rousing
"Ode on the Sailing of Our Troops for France," dedicated it
to Wilson, and published it in the *North American Review*
(November, 1917). World War I was "a sacramental feast
. . . Which to have died in were enough of life."[12] Turned
journalist-morale builder, he published war essays in the
Atlantic Monthly, the *Outlook,* and the *North American
Review*; carried on a massive correspondence; and agitated in
conversation. He believed that to suffer was to grow; it was
but human nature. The League of Nations was his hope that
suffering through war could be eliminated.

The war effort had cost Chapman much in life energy, in
the loss of his son, and in the diminishing of his willed
optimism. This was his period of *mezzo cammin,* what his
biographer M. A. DeWolfe Howe appropriately called the
period of banked fires. Chapman wrote some labored essays
and collected his poems for publication. The sense of his
own years, the estimate of his energies, and the tiredness that
recalled the *Nursery* times he expressed in "Sonnet on Middle
Life":

> Trouble thyself no more. The time is brief.
> Thy mind is harvested: its little sheaf
> Stands in the granary of yesterday.[13]

But he did not take his own advice. He may have faltered,
but he did not stop. Between 1919-32 he published nine
books. But he did feel disoriented in the new epoch of the
1920's, for it was not the world he had grown up in. He tried
in various ways to understand it. His habits sustained him.
Once a reformer, always a reformer. Ideas were weapons even
as politics were tactics. Keeping up his reading in several
languages and concentrating his interest in education and
religion, Chapman's interest in politics waned.[14] Social issues
broader than politics needed to be practically agitated. He

carried on a small pamphlet war on Prohibition, attacking the tyranny of the dogma that a bad law could implement a dubious cause. In the manner of Thoreau and Emerson, Chapman could be only optionally obedient to the law, providing the law agreed (as Antigone had felt) with conscience. He could not be indifferent; he had to take a side. He published forced rather than forceful essays in the *North American Review*, the *Outlook*, the *Independent*, and the *New Republic* linking drink, Sophocles, and *Hamlet*. (Chapman was at this time an "angel" to Walter Hampden's dramatic productions.)

VI *His Politics Persist in Protest*

True, Chapman's skill in political definition abated, but he never abandoned his determined impulse to speak out. The right to articulate rebellion was to him inalienable. It was the private self against the Maxim silencer of society, institutions, custom, law, might which certainly did not make right, and the many who certainly, too, could be wrong. And, of course, he could be wrong.

Thus far in his causes Chapman had been more right than wrong. Nostalgia for the homogeneous world of his Dutchess County, New York, caused him to view with alarm the dying out of social life in America. Washington Square was now full of foreigners. Immigration was at fault. The Anglo-Saxon tradition was in danger of being lost, Gino Speranza mourned in *Race or Nation* (1925); and, in reviewing it for the *Yale Review* (April, 1926), Chapman agreed. Chapman was worried, like Tom Buchanan in *The Great Gatsby*. It was not, Chapman insisted, that he wanted to add fuel to the mounting fires of hostile racial and religious antagonisms in America, but America was more than the land of gold the immigrants thought it was; the ghettos of mass aliens should be dispersed; and common secondary and adult education should be made compulsory. Now to Chapman the solution of political problems—when the solution was not specifically religious—was in education. Political education as he had defined it in

Practical Agitation was enveloped in, almost completely disguised by, the larger views of education, religion, and literature he wrote about. (These matters are explored in subsequent chapters.)

Chapman did not abandon his habit of protest, for to speak out was not only the signal of courage and practical agitation but also an act of education. Chapman spoke out on darker fears: mass immigration had increased the number and power of Roman Catholics and Jews in America. The first fear had been a long smoldering family cause; the second, though considerably more ancient, had in the 1920's a fashionable and contemporary international circulation, even in the poetry of T. S. Eliot. In *Notes on Religion* (1915), Chapman had made out a case of evil consequences arising out of the cause of authoritarian rule by the Roman Church, a corruption no more hypothetical than that of a railroad going through a city as he had even earlier pointed out in *Causes and Consequences.* Although George Santayana in his review of *Notes* in the *New Republic* (January 15, 1916) demurred, he did not change Chapman's mind. Ten years later the machinery of the Roman Church still irked Chapman the independent, the separatist, the non-conformist Christian. He argued with a Catholic sister-in-law, wrote angry letters to newspapers, accused Harvard of catering to Catholics, and stirred up controversy in Irish-Catholic Boston and in the pages of *Commonweal.*

He claimed he was only speaking out whereas the Ku Klux Klan's clandestine activity was discrediting a real cause.[15] He carried his burden to a six-months' paper war in the *Forum* magazine in which he aired his prejudices about the KKK, Catholic presidential candidate Alfred E. Smith, and the mealy-mouthed avoidance of American thought on these questions. Further inflamed, he even published a sonnet in the KKK journal, the *National Kourier,* to disseminate his inflamed feelings against the Jesuits and Jews who were landing near Plymouth and were intent upon wrecking America.[16] It was a sonnet, passionate, misinformed, and misguided.

Chapman's fitful feelings left no permanent disfigurement either on the times or upon himself. His political agitation—a lifelong attitude and practice—unified his life. This fact resolves Edmund Wilson's difficulty in seeing Chapman's life as a whole. Toward the end of his life, Chapman's political protest had spent itself on unrewarding causes. As early as 1901 he saw that the mirror of politics was old and cracked; its reflections were distorted and unreliable. But he continued to use it. He abandoned many but not all of the graceless controversies and turned instead to literary and educational opinion-making and to the consolation of his private religious pieties. In a sense, every book he wrote was a piece of education, and every one he wrote was equally of religious and spiritual intention and import. The breadth and intricacy of his interests necessitate looking at the imperatives of his mind and the disputes that created his books now as politics, now as education, again as a matter of religion, and still again as a work of literary criticism.

What, according to Chapman, was the condition of education in America?

CHAPTER 4

The Blackboard of Education

TO KNOW IS TO BE, but the best I must own of knowing or being it is TO BE KNOWN.[1] Thus, satirically, in Chapman's first published book, he mounted his first attack on educators. (His last published book was also concerned with education.) In the slender "sad, quaint comedy" entitled *The Two Philosophers,* whose matter was trivial, whose verse was little better than doggerel, whose drama was negligible, Chapman dealt an Aristophanic blow to two cloud-like Harvard philosophy professors: Josiah Royce and F. E. Abbott. He ridiculed the philosophers' self-glorification as they went about ticketing ideas, their dogmatism, their specialism, and their obtrusive vanity of putting themselves between the thing to be known and the learners. The vital thing was that the blackboard must not be obstructed. Education had so much to do with things unseen that anything that hampered the process was critical. Between 1892 and 1932, the date of *New Horizons in American Life,* Chapman tried to keep the blackboard in clear view.

The Two Philosophers foreshadows the line of Chapman's thinking. In a basic sense every book he wrote was preceptive —a piece of education. The *Nursery* was a primer to the politically befuddled, corrupt, and apathetic. *Causes and Consequences* and *Practical Agitation* contained explicit chapters on education, on Froebel (cited by Rugg as a strong influence on the theory of progressive education), and on the moral and civic value of pondering the daily affairs of one's town or city. His plays for children were sugar-coated moralities. Specific essays on school matters were contained in *Learning and Other Essays* and in *Memories and Milestones*. His translations of Homer and Sophocles, his book on Dante, his essays on Lucian and Plato, and his book on Shakespeare were all meant to correct what he alleged were faulty classroom accents in teaching those subjects. His two books on religious matters were devotional books containing Chapman's instruction on the imitation of Christ. His literary criticism (especially of Emerson) and his biography of Garrison (and the many charming brief memoirs he wrote) were frankly inspirational. They were attempted popularizations designed to rescue great men from little critics, smaller biographers, and the anonymity of country churchyards. Just as there is no evidence that Chapman desired public or official political office, similarly there is no evidence that he desired academic position. He was, nevertheless, recognized as an educator-at-large: Hobart and Yale conferred honorary degrees upon him, and his essays were included in college textbooks. His lifelong concern with education continued the long family tradition of active support of educational enterprises.

Chapman himself was introspectively aware of the processes of his own education, for he recorded in letter and book his griefs and exaltations with formal education. Until adolescence he had had no regular schooling or tutoring. His *Retrospections* tells how heavily the surcharged religiousness of St. Paul's school life marked him, edging him into illness and withdrawal. He entered Harvard with a background of personal and private education gleaned from tutors, travel, and browsing in the libraries of parents and grandparents; he had also a miscellaneous knowledge of art, music, drama, and the classics casually acquired while wandering around the theaters, museums, and bookstalls of New York City. With his self-awareness, as his letters of this period testify, Chapman was literally jolted by the books he read, by the teachers he had, and by the varied education which cultured Boston was capable of dispensing. He could, indeed, get an education there if he wanted one; he wanted one.

Classes were small. The professors were approachable and

amiable. The Harvard paladins of those days included Charles
Eliot Norton, William W. Goodwin, George M. Lane, Josiah
Royce, William James, Nathaniel S. Shaler, George H. Palmer,
Francis J. Child, and George Lyman Kittredge. Chapman
remembered them all his life, and his memory of some of them
he etched with acid:

> Professor Child . . . was an old-fashioned, caustic, witty
> little fellow of the Scotch type, the headlight of modern
> Teutonic scholarship in America, and his subject was
> Ballads. His attitude toward the students was Peck-
> sniffian. . . . He became for me the symbol of the
> German school of documentation, classification and foot-
> notes. Kittredge was his pupil, and Kittredge was an
> iron man who would be seen stalking about Cambridge
> with a vicious looking small bag filled with burglar's
> tools and footnotes on Othello. I looked with a shudder
> on both Child and Kittredge and to this day feel that
> between the commentaries of such men and the works of
> genius to which they tag their notes, there is a deep
> gulf fixed.[2]

While attending Harvard College, Chapman's sensibilities
were stirred and his tastes and interests fixed. They were
fortified comparatively and critically by his many European
trips, but they were not seriously affected by his subsequent
studies in law, though he relished the Socratic method of law
case class instruction. When we consider all the subjects of
his books, we note that there is no published essay on law
or legal matters.

With marriage and children came naturally Chapman's
interest in the education of his sons; they, too, went to St.
Paul's School and Harvard. He spoke from various college
rostrums. From a distance he carried on a letter and pamphlet
war against the changing complexion of Harvard University.
Like Oliver Wendell Holmes, he read occasional poems to
anniversary meetings of his class of 1884. He corresponded
over the years with many educators and scholars in America,
England, France, and even in Japan: Nicholas Murray Butler

(Columbia), Arthur T. Hadley (Yale), William James, Émile Legouis, A. Lawrence Lowell, John Livingston Lowes, Robert Nichols (an English poet who later taught in Japan), William Amory Gardner (patron of the Groton School), C. B. Tinker, J. E. Spingarn, Henry Osborn Taylor, George McLean Harper, and headmasters of private schools. Many of these letters reflect Chapman's passion for neglected excellence in American education; and, because he was committed so strongly to his point of view, many of the controversies he participated in were in their day acrimonious. Education to Chapman, like politics, was promises. He was disturbed when promises were compromised by cheapness, shoddiness, and a lack of understanding of the perspective of America's projected greatness. Nothing less than America's democracy was at stake. A perfected democracy was our horizon.

New Horizons in American Life shows Chapman in his consistent development and reflects the drift of tendency and approach over the past seventy-five years in treating the multi-faceted problems of educating an American population moving toward the two hundred million mark. To the generations who were to build universities around the cyclotron, to erect skyscraper schools of business, and who would be in danger of succumbing to the aggressive claims of managerial science, commercialism, and practical success, Chapman pointed out the older claims of the traditional ideals of education upon intellect and character. Upon Chapman's blackboard of education were written the same images he had seen when he had looked into the mirror of politics.

America's Gilded Age, as reckoned in conventional history books, coincided with the adult Chapman's early life. According to his own books, it lasted all his life; and, were he still alive, he would undoubtedly say it was still continuing. In his two books of political observations at the turn of the century,— *Causes and Consequences* and *Practical Agitation*—he had demonstrated the relationship between politics and commercialism that had intimidated the American people. In his observations on American educational changes during his lifetime he saw the teaming-up of applied science and commercialism which was intimidating the teacher and bemusing the learner. (He had but to mention the capture of engineering by government, and he would have identified the stupendous post-World War II Nuclear Age-Space-Missile developments of our time.) True, industrial development had to come, and America was merely the outstanding example of this industrial expansion dominated by commercialism. Business and applied science imperatives pre-empted the minds and purposes of the tycoon, philanthropist, and man-in-the-street. Education reflected too well this historical development. This observation was the core of "Our Universities," his first chapter in *New Horizons.*

In the transformation of universities from shanty to skyscraper, crass and unimaginatively utilitarian business ideals had warped the curriculum, deadened the textbooks, saddled the teacher with mechanized lesson schedules and the drudgery of decimal marking systems, inflated the certification value of a doctorate, and proliferated arid monographs by and for equally arid scholars. The terrible Teutonism of men like Child and Kittredge had visibly triumphed. The dogmas of science and business—bigness, efficiency, success—were lethal to the impulses and achievements of the arts and humanities. After all, the Bible, Greek drama, Dante, Balzac, Shakespeare, Emerson, and Garrison were not products of any calculating machine or laboratory that Chapman knew of.

What was needed in 1932, and more than ever because of America's involvement in Europe during and after World War I, was an education that underlined and fulfilled the simple fact that all men are brothers: "This is an age when any man must feel embarrassed to find himself on a platform, booked to preach on what is in everyone's mind—war, peace, science, religion, art, industry, social life—for they all point today to the same text on the blackboard, to the impending unification of human life upon the globe: 'Ye are members one of another.' "[3]

Gone from Chapman's mind was the hysteria of his

propaganda book, *Deutschland über Alles,* the flag waving that accompanied the American Expeditionary Forces to Europe, the fear of immigrant millions in America, and the mourning for his dead aviator son. He saw the numerous international conferences and the spate of news dispatches and feature articles in American newspapers and magazines as information linking intellectually skimpy America with the rich treasure of the European past. The educational consequences of increased traffic with Europe would show up, he predicted, in our daily reading, writing, and conversation.

What Chapman was saying in 1932 to his college audience was a significant and revealing variation of what he had said in 1900 to another college audience when he addressed the graduating class of Hobart College. Fresh from the reform battles on the sidewalks of New York City, he told his Geneva, New York, audience of college seniors' that politics was a way of realizing the unity of human nature. The need in politics was for young men to speak *for* principle and to speak *against* the gag-rule of timidity that aborted the process of self-government. To do so was to speak symbolically; in effect, it was to testify to the watching world (China, Africa, Russia) that practical democracy is—in historical perspective— America's contribution to the advancement of the human condition. It was an optimistic view he offered:

> Democracy thus lets character loose upon society. . . . In America the young man meets the struggle between good and evil in the easiest form in which it was ever laid before men. The cruelties of interest and of custom have with us no artificial assistance from caste, creed, race prejudice. . . . By our documents we are dedicated to mankind; and hence it is that we can so easily feel the pulse of the world and lay our hand on the living organism of humanity.[4]

The spirit of the speech echoed his remark of this same period that it was better to cast a vote than to write a book. Thus, America could teach Europe. By 1932 when his political activism abated, he was still sure that America could teach the world democracy by example, but now it needed the substance of the culture of Europe to make us feel the unity of human nature. Europe could still teach us. The history of Europe included the Classics, Christianity, and the Revival of Learning. Involvement with Europe meant these, too.

Experience with the humanities of Europe could only be salutary. It would correct the yaw, roll, and torque of the American business machine as it hurtled through civilization. To be sure, Ben Franklin's virtues of thrift, social improvement, and community life were determinants of America's history; but there had been another period in our history— the epoch of Abolitionism—that had revealed the Christian, moral energies of America as more characteristic than Franklin's. That time had revealed a horizon for moral progress to the American at home and to the world. With post-World War I America involved in Europe, the opportunity was at hand for America to disavow its isolationism and to get involved with the more historied, more culturally complex humanistic mind of Europe. American "know-how" was what Europe needed to rehabilitate itself; but the respect of Europe for the past of man was just what was needed by Americans to correct their timidity, uniformity, and conformity.

> Let us admit our deficiencies. The difference between European cultivation and our own is a difference in complexity. Theirs has more resonances, more overtones. It stirs thicker. There are more threads to an inch in the tapestry. . . . But our democracy terrifies the individual, and our industrialism seals his lips. . . . The uniformity of the popular ideals and ambitions in America is at the bottom of most of our troubles.[5]

Twenty-five years before Riesman, Glazer, and Denney's *The Lonely Crowd*, Chapman diagnosed the changing American character and made his prognosis.

Education was practical agitation for the life according to character and intellect. In the style of Emerson and with the

confidence of William James, Chapman put the matter to
the test of experience and time:

> Our political life is undergoing rapid transformations, and
> the chat on street corners is more free. You are alarmed
> at the coarseness and feebleness of our journals? It is
> better than silence. You grieve at their multiplicity? This
> is nature's way. She tries experiments and thus finds out
> which germ will grow and which will not. . . . But you
> say, "How can we tell in which direction the whole
> process is tending?" Only by the outcome.[6]

It is clear that despite the book's pragmatic exit, it was not
helpful and specific in the sense that the works—particular and
prescriptive—of Randolph Bourne, John Dewey, Abraham
Flexner, and George S. Counts were in those days. But the
point should not be lost that Chapman insisted that, within
the steel skeleton and behind the glass walls of our skyscraper schools, there must be a heart-moving and mind-
warming involvement with a time-demonstrated principle.
Man, a creature but slightly lower than the angels, deserves
an education worthy of his rung of the ladder. Chapman's
protest against anything less came out of his militant Protestantism. His insistence upon morality in politics was of a
piece with his insistence upon idealism in education. The
onset of the worldwide economic depression of the 1930's
and the accelerated programs of aggressive fascism and
communism were not assessed in Chapman's *New Horizons*.
His was a minority voice faintly heard in the din of a world
of masses in militant motion and entangled in the complexities
of mass communications, propaganda, and calculated prepara-
tions for another devastating war.

Chapman's exhortation to the devices of inwardness, to the
self-reliance that comes from deeply inculcated morality and
idealism, placed him, unofficially, among the neo-Humanist
critics of the early part of the twentieth century. He had known
the neo-Humanist literature in its uncollected, nascent,
magazine period, especially as it appeared in the pages of the

Atlantic Monthly in which his early essays had been published. In articles of the 1890's, W. P. Trent, Basil Gildersleeve, and Irving Babbitt had decried the academic tendency toward philological-historical literary criticism, the neglect of the classics, and the overestimation of the Romantic, the Realistic, and the Naturalistic in literature. Such advices strengthened Chapman in his distaste for both the monographs that ravaged learning and the journalistic treatments that betrayed it. Furthermore, his sustained preoccupation with Greek literature tempered his equally sustained insistence upon the priority of the content of Hebraism in Western culture. Like Matthew Arnold, Chapman's ideal curriculum was a practical synthesis of Hellenism and Hebraism, the Beauty of one balancing the Good of the other, with both culminating in Truth. Wherever these ideals indicated imbalance, Chapman criticized the responsible men and institutions. Chapman tried to keep his own admiration for the Hebraism of New England in correct perspective.

For instance, back in 1898, in the *Nursery* he attacked Harvard's Charles Eliot Norton for his parochial, Puritan, Boston view that there was no polish in America, except stove polish.[7] Chapman's Knickerbocker origins and loyalties were set against Boston dictation. The gist of his objection was that the Puritan strain inhibited art in America; and Harvard, certainly, was not the authoritative voice of America. On this point he was at one with Poe and he anticipated the anti-Puritanism of H. L. Mencken, Van Wyck Brooks, and Lewis Mumford.

The dogmatism of Harvard and the dogmas of its professors and president—William James, Hugo Munsterberg, Charles W. Eliot—irked him. Dogmatism was a variety of imbalance. President Eliot's hope for education for the millions had led him to expand Harvard and to attract endowments. This expansion to Chapman spelled the pursuit of quantity not quality and could only bode ill for the future of college education in America. Chapman's aristophilism, his upper-class sympathies, and his cultivated gentlemanliness conditioned severely his large view of democratic education in America. This noted, it must be added to his credit that his insistence upon excellence in teacher, student, and institution is a matter only recently underscored by the "population explosion" as it affects all levels of American education.

Like Lincoln Steffens, Chapman believed there was little in formal education that could help a man to see life steadily and whole. But, unlike Steffens and more like Emerson, Chapman insisted that the religious view of life with its inherent disavowal of self-interest was educational. It pierced the apparent mysteries of behavior. Just as greedy self-interest had no honorable juncture with the making of the good man, it had no place in the behavior of a university. Thus, when by formal vote Harvard granted the use of its name to the promotion of the famous five-foot shelf series, the *Harvard Classics* (edited by Charles W. Eliot, LL.D., complete with Harvard seal), Chapman fumed. Harvard had capitulated to department store ideas, cash register values, and commercialism: "Eliot and Harvard have become mere trademarks. We shall likely live to see their names on collar-boxes—a picture of Eliot, a box of soap and a set of the *Harvard Classics*."[8]

Unpleasant as the appearance of the spirit of grab was at Harvard, the spectacle of intimidated teachers was worse. In "Professorial Ethics," published earlier in a magazine and collected in *Learning and Other Essays* (1910), Chapman scored the professor's timidity in not defending one of his group from expulsion from a university and in taking dictation of curricular policies not from fellow scholars but from administrative superiors who were preoccupied with the business of learning and not with learning. Business and the ethos of business were clearly insinuating themselves into American colleges and were, worse, compromising the integrity of the teachers. The "boss" of politics and of business had bred the academic "boss." It was to be twenty-five years before the national American Association of University Professors (founded in 1914, it had only 50,000 members in

1962) was able to support militantly and effectively Chapman's espousal of academic freedom not only against the encroachments of a businessman's orthodoxy demanded of teachers but also against the illegalities of political orthodoxy in a climate of oppressive investigating committees, House Un-American Activities Committee, and citizens' vigilante surveillance. Chapman's essay also anticipated Upton Sinclair, who quoted from it in his muckraking study of higher education in America, *The Goose-step* (1923).

Chapman's definition of education cannot be reduced to an easily memorized slogan. Its properties were too volatile, or electric, or coruscating, or fiery; they were always in process of becoming something else. This is apparent in "Learning," the title essay of *Learning and Other Essays,* an essay that had the advantage of a wide circulation in the *Atlantic Monthly* (July, 1910) and that caught the appreciative eye of John Dewey. It revealed the living center of Chapman's passionate intellectualism that made him the culture critic—the man of ideas that he was.

Learning made Chapman reverential. A thinking mind was an exquisite delight. A thinking mind guaranteed the perpetuation of tradition, which is time caught in a poem, a play, a vase, a building. Yet tradition is experimental and tentative; the learner senses the utterance or gesture of the admired work and is liberated to try his talent, thereby joining an ever-incomplete tradition. The temporal events of American life—the traumas of colonial settlement and revolution, the surge of sudden wealth, and the acclamation accorded to gadgetry of uninspired science—increasingly turned American education against the thrill of intellectual quest. Their effect was to isolate America from the mind of the past. But the law of the world was the unity of human nature—not isolation in it, and certainly not insulation against it. "I do not recommend subserviency to Europe," he wrote, "but subserviency to intellect."[9] Intellect had cracked the obvious tyrannies of the past; intellect could depose the subtle tyrannies of the present. Intellect flowed through the universe.

The task of teaching and the joy of learning were to tap the inexhaustible reservoir of invisible influence around man in his universe of discourse. In this way Chapman called for renovation, for reconstruction: for "the birth of a new spirit and of a new philosophic attitude in our university life."

Now, no one can precisely gauge the effect of an exhortation that touches us. Chapman's affirmations kindled others beside Dewey, Abraham Flexner, and Randolph Bourne to sense the unexpended potential of American education. Perhaps it helped to stir Van Wyck Brooks's *America's Coming-of-Age* (1915) to its influential existence. What Chapman had written was an exploration of the low-middle-high brow culture controversy of the past fifty years. C. P. Snow's nagging worry about the lack of communication between the two cultures of the arts and sciences, expressed in *The Two Cultures and the Scientific Revolution* (1959), is a recent instance.

The humanism of Chapman's goals of education was not expressed in generalized jeremiads. Education had consequences and applications to areas seemingly remote from schooling. Specifically, what had education to do with race relations in America? Everything, said Chapman. Among the miscellaneous essays in *Memories and Milestones* Chapman included "The Negro Question," a speech he had delivered to the New York Chapter of the National Association for the Advancement of Colored People. In it he expressed the now familiar notion that education could accomplish the ultimate amelioration of Negro-white animosities and cruelties in America:

> Since 1870, the Negro question has ceased to be the pivot upon which our whole civilization turned, and has sunk to the position of being the chief among the great problems before us. It is a problem that has been clearly recognized and is being nobly met by the whites and the blacks alike. Christianity, training, and education—these things are the solution, these things are the need of all of us. If we keep our individual minds clear of all rancor, time will do the rest.[10]

It is precisely the broad, franchise-conferring power of education that white supremacists instinctively fear; it has made school integration during the last ten years the lens through which we see Negro-white relations in America.

Over the next seventeen years (1915-32) Chapman continued to observe the drift of education. He kept up a running commentary in essays, in book reviews, in letters to the editor, in private correspondence, and in college lecture hall. He discovered no new causes, but rather found accumulating evidence of the abuses he had earlier attacked and the hopes he nurtured. He kept his eye on the development of the private school, watched warily lest Harvard commit more public follies, signaled strenuously his anxieties over the noticeable growth of religious school education and his fears about Roman Catholic expansion in America, advocated more attention to the gifted child as an antidote to mediocrity, praised in artful memoir the achievements of cultivated people, and optimistically searched the horizon for sure signs of rising literacy in energetic America. He praised dissenters, encouraged satire, and pleaded for the minority of intellectuals in America ("shut-ins of culture," he called them).

His essay, "The Unity of Human Nature," found its way into a freshman English reader, *College and the Future* (1915), edited by Richard Rice, Jr.—the first of its appearances in a half-dozen anthologies. In 1916, along with artist John Singer Sargent and classical scholar Charles Allen Dinsmore, Chapman was awarded an honorary Doctor of Letters degree by Yale University. After 1918 he hoped that one of the beneficial results of the defeat of Germany might be the casting off of the graduate school admiration for the imported method of German historical-scientific literary criticism that turned artistic analysis into a bore.

In the 1920's he made fun of an accomplished fact. He had feared the inroads of commercialism upon American colleges. Now the very atmosphere of university learning was disturbed by a new breed of men—expert income appraisers, trained publicity men, tribes of alumni gladhanders—whose talk was of sports, whose ideal was social mixing in the name of "service," and whose passion was to keep stocks above par. Chapman ridiculed the college-development men, the professional boosters. He projected a satirical picture of Harvard clubbiness: Harvard graduates would be offered the opportunity of being buried only among Harvard men.

Chapman was not appeased when Harvard men defended the newly established Harvard School of Business in language familiar to house-organ releases of the National Association of Manufacturers. He was sure our "well-to-do, ingenuous, socially ambitious, and intellectually vacant industrial class" was destroying the schools, the curriculum, and the spur to excellence that was learning. In the New York *Times Book Review* he lamented the prevalence of slovenly thinking and writing; they were products of our failure in attention "which a large class of Americans will not give to any book except a ledger."

He insisted that he was not campaigning to get automobiles off Fifth Avenue, nor stockbrokers out of club windows; he was not attacking democracy. His aim was to stave off the degradation of the American intellect. On rare occasions—like the establishment of the Graduate School at Princeton and the quiet, unpublicized work of private schools like Phillips Andover, St. Mark's School, Groton—did education refuse to answer "the Call of the Wild—Business."[11] How could one expect the immigrant millions of America's past forty years to resist the siren call of what his dear friend William James described as "the bitch goddess Success" if the schools did not teach them to resist?[12]

Chapman's lifelong defense of the Protestant private school, art school, and of the humanities against the mounting popularity of vocational education might be construed as the position of a conservative, even reactionary, in education. Semantically, it would be better to consider him a conservationist. Chapman was not victimized by the myth of nostalgia. He saw, rather, that the reality of educational process lacked principle. It was expedient, serving the expediencies of temporal success. The classroom blackboards were filled with the doodles of business arithmetic, the calculations of commerce. But character and intellect transcended the temporal creature comforts and vulgarities of mass society in which the individual was sacrificed for gross production, statistically defined. Education should be a tool of power energizing the individual to live his daily life addressed to the responsibility of literacy and voting, the responsibility for lynching and war, and the responsibility to one world of creatures made in a divine image. This last statement is literally the vital clue to the organic configuration of Chapman's views on education.

His admiration for the Mediterranean classics has already been mentioned. His remark, "It is easier to imagine a substitute for telegraphy than a substitute for Horace's *Odes*," is the hyperbole of a professing Humanist.[13] When we consider Chapman's avowals, in *Notes on Religion* and in *Letters and Religion*, of his strong, profound allegiance to the Bible and then add Christian to his Humanism, the consistent strength of the source of his educational criticism is revealed. In 1897 he had written in a letter:

> I read the Bible all the time and carry it about when I don't read it, I don't know why. It is the only power and opening of one's self. . . . I'm glad I'm a Jew. I believe that's the reason why this paper-faced civilization impresses me so little. . . . Greek literature would have lived if it had any such human touch and bang in it [as in some cited verses from Habakkuk]. . . . It is inconceivable that anything should be closer to life than the Old Testament—but the New Testament is much closer.[14]

Twenty-five years later he had not changed his mind:

> And here let us pause for a moment and watch the glowing shadow of the Christian religion as it passes across the face of our civilization. I began this essay by talking about books and bookishness, and the influences of humanism in its larger sense; and the discussion has

led us to the Bible, which is the best example we have
to show the importance of reading and writing in human
life. . . . Of all the media of communication between man
and man, the Bible is the greatest mind-touching influence
that swallows us unto union with God and with all men,
dispelling the crass illusions of the moment, leading us to
rely on the unseen.[15]

In summary, Chapman's lifelong preoccupation with education was critical but optimistic. America's accelerated development of material culture had its hidden taxes: the somewhat gaudy product, after all, was shoddily constructed.
America could disregard the content of European culture no
more than the Renaissance could have disregarded the Graeco-
Roman civilization, than the Christian his Jewish predecessors,
and, ultimately, no more than man the God who had created
him. The heritage of American ethical idealism that was born
in the colonial settlement, invigorated during the American
Revolution, tested in the Civil War, submerged in the Gilded
Age, and further refined in World War I was in our post-war
connection with Europe reunited with its source. Our peculiar
nationalism would merge with internationalism. But Humanism with its sense of the past and its active desire to educate
the young in the uses of the past was the common denominator
of both "isms." Education was influence, and influence was
education. Small classes, the salon atmosphere where talk
was encouraged, support of art schools and private schools
where experimentation can go on, unintimidated teachers, the
Socratic method of instruction, texts oriented to the humanities,
the fostering of handicrafts—these were a few of his recommended devices.

These devices put a constructive value on the worth of the
individual—the agent of Chapman's intellectual democracy
of virtue and talent. He himself was an individual among
individuals who had helped Harvard over the years to become more democratic. For his constructive criticism he was
praised by Porter Sargent, Harvard '96 (characterized by the

Harvard *Crimson* as the "dyspeptic surveyor of the preparatory school"), in Sargent's famous *Handbook*. Sargent put Chapman into company with Emerson, Wendell Phillips, Charles Francis Adams, and Nathaniel Shaler.[16] Chapman was, of course, more to education than a gad-fly to Harvard. His books continue to excite thought and to provoke other critics, like Jacques Barzun, to publish praise of intellect and to encourage independence in teachers. In the 1960's America came face-to-face with the look of crisis in education. Not numbers but the quality of educator and educated is the nub of the question. The role of education in a responsive democracy largely controls the destiny of the people on this earth, except those seduced by the dubious attractions of a militant totalitarianism.

Chapman's signal service to education was to refuse to be overawed or distracted by the American penchant for "jumboism" (painfully reflected in grandiose educational development plans on jumbo billboards at campus gates). He refused to take his attention away either from the blackboard, the teacher, and the student or from the fugue, vase, or sonnet the teacher pointed to as he tried to elucidate the mystery of mind. Chapman's reverence for the mystery of mind qualified his opinions about philosophy, psychology, and science in America. Any attempt to freeze, solidify, inhibit, or in any way rigorize the flow of spirit in things was anti-education. And the most notorious sappers of education were philosophers, social scientists, and scientists. He made them special targets of his fun and disbelief.

CHAPTER 5

The Deceptions of Dogma

CHAPMAN hated fences as much as Rousseau or any other instinctively freeborn trespasser. They should never be erected; but, if erected, it was one's duty to agitate against them so that they might be cast down. Metaphysical philosophy, organized science, institutional religion, and systematic theology had this in common: they were all demonstrably and dangerously liable to the building of fences. The word game of modern philosophy, the Church's historical patents on certain ideas, the confusion of means and ends, of sacred and profane, in ecclesiastical practice, the saying of more than one knows or is known (which was Chapman's definition of theology in *Letters and Religion*)—these were to him kinds of fences, varieties of dogma. Being much less than the truth, they deceive. And what, possibly, could God have to do with deception?

When he published the energetic *Nursery*, he, with a poker face, blazoned on the mast of all issues: "The object of THE NURSERY is to tell the truth. There is no publication at present which seems to cover this exact field." He had one in mind, however, one other than the *Nursery*. It was not a publication. It was a book. But it had no dogma in it. It was the Bible. The Bible displaced all the philosophy he read during his life, measured science and the emerging social sciences of his lifetime, and served him as touchstone to test civilization. With it he went out to appraise his world in more than twenty-five books; to it he returned time and again for consolation, inspiration, and recuperation. It supplied him with the directive sense of unity in a lifetime of overtly miscellaneous causes.

To watch him define his consciousness of the adventure of self-in-history is to watch him refine the religious sensibilities of his family inheritance and the vicissitudes of his private life. Family religious values had been ingrained in him before he tallied them; schooling intensified them; his intellectualism tested them in the age of Social Darwinism; and grievous experience in the valleys of death and prostrating illnesses drove him painfully deep into himself seeking re-sources within reach for optimistic persistence in living. His consciousness of God, beginning when he could not say, was an incalculable force in his life. *Letters and Religion,* a spiritual biography, recorded how religion had bound him to life and how it had made him free. If it had done this for him, it could do so for others. Not ritual, propaganda, or dogma had done this for him, but rather his awareness when he read, say, the story and sayings of Christ. Then he was caught in the running currents of the universe. It gave him his identity as a human being desiring the best of humanity for himself and, it followed, for others. The words and conduct of Christ liberated Chapman, not the doctrine or dogma the Church had made of them. It was pristine Christianity he sought all his life. It was neither the Church nor the cowl he sought; it was Christness.

As a fourth-generation Jay and a second-generation Chap-man, John Jay Chapman had bitter memories of Huguenot steadfastness in the face of Jesuit persecution and poignant memories of the messianic movement that was Abolitionism. Had not the Jays taken the stump in New York and in Indianapolis against the Roman Church? Had not Grand-mother Chapman written fervent hymns to Christ the Abolitionist? Had not Grandfather Chapman abandoned the Unitarian ministry in protest against its lukewarm yea-and nay-saying? The piety of both families—family devotions, Bible reading, American Bible Society affairs—worked its way into the boy's habits. The two family traditions reinforced each other warp and woof. The Jay tradition was the triple tradition of the Constitution, the law courts, and the Bible; the Chapman tradition was the Garrison-defiance of the Constitution and the law courts and the appeal to the Bible as the higher authority.

To this upbringing the ravages of real and psychosomatic illness, the pathology of desperate decisions, the sudden death of Minna Chapman, the drowning of Jay, the death of Victor, the circumstantial failures of his political reforms, the depravity of lynching, the holocaust of war, and the persistent cupidity of man in his root-and-branch activities periodically fatigued Chapman, bankrupting temporarily his idealism. His nature was preponderantly intuitive. His emotions were poised delicately, even, dangerously, close to his senses. Emerson's line from "The Problem" applies to Chapman: "Himself from God he could not free." Nor did he want to be free of God. The family motto welcomed suffering as a way of learning.

As a boy, he read religious books like Coleridge's *Aids to Reflection,* later he was neurotically affected by the pietistic atmosphere and regimen of St. Paul's School, and he was still further agitated by music. Heard melodies were sweet: he could cry at *Lohengrin;* it was like a "deification" to hear Schubert's *Unfinished Symphony* and like taking a bath in Elysium to have heard Mozart's *Don Giovanni.*[1] Yet, unheard melodies were painfully sweeter: "I have had a revelation—Robert Browning. You will smile—fact all the same. I read him till daybreak—and cried."[2] Chapman was then twenty-one years old.

Chapman's first wife, Minna, was a young woman whose religiousness and sensitivity to mystical matters reinforced his own tendencies. Chapman so described her in the preface to *Victor Chapman's Letters from France.* His law work pleased him less than reading the Bible: "O these law books. . . . Set 'em up one way you have a sword. Set 'em up another way you have a shield. This is the whole law—and the prophets are in a different department."[3] The triangle of the Bible, his emotions, and Minna enclosed him. He was happy. After Minna's death, reading the Bible—"the only power and opening of one's self"—consoled him.

I *Christian Humanist*

If Chapman during the decade 1890-1900 had depended upon the power of political instruments to guide social reform, if Chapman had planned to invest the neglected classics with the power of resolving our social difficulties, if Chapman had advocated a boot-strap Humanism as the way out, by 1901 he thought so no longer. The classicist had changed into the Christian, the Humanist into the Christian Humanist. The riddle of the "power and opening of one's self" was in the lilies of the field:

> Bear your sorrows into the fields—
> Sympathy their silence yields
> Deeper than mankind can give thee
> For they know not and they care not,
> And they pry not and they stare not,
> But with green religion growing,
> Their unconsciousness bestowing,
> Carelessly accepted, receive thee.[4]

His rod and His staff, henceforth—no matter how concealed they might be—were to be in the phrase "green religion growing." Like William Cullen Bryant whose significant adjective is green and like Whitman whose cosmic mysticism is suggested in the recurrent cycle of green grass, Chapman cultivated a personal, mystical ever-changing yet ever-constant confidence in the shaping force behind the forms of things. Dogma, which does not grow, was a kind of death-in-life. He would celebrate growing, becoming, unfolding, and opening; he would attack all those who inhibited the right tendency in things. His performance may appear to be erratic, even in instances misguided. It certainly did not impede philosophical speculation in America, nor inhibit the growth of giant science in America; but it does illustrate the fretful search for religious meaning in the advancing secular American life of the early part of the twentieth century.

The significance of his anonymously published satire on two Harvard teachers of philosophy, *The Two Philosophers,* was that it set the tone for Chapman's rebuke to that tribe of men who had made a new word game, a crossword puzzle for adults, out of their pursuit of the meaning of God. Chapman talked with Charles Pierce and pretended he did not understand his profundity; he repudiated the life built on the negations of Schopenhauer and Nietzsche; he regretted that Kant had been misused by modern philosophers who were using his words at second hand, dabbling where he had played for high stakes; he praised much in Plato, in Dante's use of Aquinas, in Henri Bergson, and in A. N. Whitehead; and he twitted his cherished friend, William James. It was William James who had the good grace to compliment Chapman as a "profound moralist" in *Varieties of Religious Experience*. It was tonic to Chapman, for he was low in spirit in 1902. Moralist Chapman was. He certainly did not like the logic chopping of philosophy.

Apart from his direct assaults upon the word-war of philosophy, he made his own activities illustrate the philosopher's quest. He sought truth through art. He wrote plays for children, read plays and poems to children at his home and in his neighborhood and to University Settlement audiences. The arts served religion even as philosophy served religion. With Mrs. Chapman (he had married Elizabeth Chanler in 1898) he tried the experiment of a clubroom in a store in Norman Thomas' sometime bailiwick, the Hell's Kitchen district of New York City. It was his custom to start the evening meetings with prayer. His prayer meeting in Coatesville was a penitential act.

When he wrote or spoke he did not publicize the latest glad tidings gleaned from the dense pages of a journal of metaphysics but the steady glimmers of an oncoming religious revival. Whereas Matthew Arnold felt that his age was to usher in a revival of poetry, Chapman thought the world was on the brink of a religious revival, an event bound to invigorate the intellect of the country. Scattered through the writings of his lifetime are qualified appreciations (regretting only the "crude dogmas and arbitrary psychology" he saw in them) of Wesleyanism, Quakerism, Ethical Culture, New Thought, Christian Science, post-war "uplift," and new horizons in education. In addition, he wrote thumb-nail sketches and graceful memoirs of New England "saints," humanitarians, teachers, and friends—all touched with the nimbus of a saint —such as William James. In substance, a sidelong glance at these activities and a steady look at man showed that man was a fool to reason about the big matters of life; psychology was a passing pseudo-science; and Freud's system was a diabolism.[5] A few years before he died, Chapman could conclude:

> My own feeling has always been that the more one's will dissolved in the Will of the Universe and the nearer one could come to the feeling of a personal relation to God, the better it was. . . . Whatever religion may be, it is a *passive* experience. . . . Religion is a thing that encloses, envelopes, and unifies, affects both the mind and the muscles, the inner and the outer—the digestion and the dreams of a man. . . . The progress of Faith on the earth seems to consist in evaporation of the capsules into which minds great and small continually strive to enclose it, and the same is true of all varieties of historical research, political theory, educational theory, etc. Poetry and the fine arts alone seem to survive the crystallization.[6]

The quest of Chapman for effective conduct and thought that ratified his religious faith was as basic to his intellectual activity as it was to his contemporary, Henry Adams. Had Chapman finished his "Retrospections," it would certainly rank higher than *The Education of Henry Adams.* Adams had the tenacity to read analytically in science, all the while yearning for an age of faith in which to live; but Chapman, impatient with both science and Henry Adams, could—and did —make the leap of faith.

[74]

Faith is a question of energy . . . a mode of motion.
It hurtles through the world and sheds doctrines, theories,
arguments, poems, pictures. . . . You think that your
machine [of faith] would have run at higher pressure
if you had lived in the Middle Ages. I see no evidence
of it. The place was full of people troubled with these
same doubts. You cannot put your finger on any age
which was not an age of transition.[7]

Addressing the International Metaphysical League in 1900
on "The Doctrine of Non-Resistance," he pronounced his
disenchantment with formal philosophy as an attack upon the
world's body, declaring himself in favor of a personal posture
of being and right doing. "Truth is a state of mind. . . . The
state of mind in which Christ lived is the truth he taught."[8]
It was precisely this—Tolstoi's own state of mind, his peasant-
mindedness and simple daily life—that won people to his
example and caused them to imitate him.[9] It certainly was
not any dogma of Tolstoi that effected this result.

Unfortunately, Chapman was decidedly ambivalent about
the injunction "Resist not evil." Fatigued, it comforted him.
His Samson-strength restored, he forgot it. Had philosophy
incorporated, let's say, outside a university, Chapman would
have gathered his strength and attacked its corporate tyranny.
Instead, he made fun of philosophers. But the Roman Church
was a corporate structure of massive dogma and power. To
Chapman, a dissident Protestant, it represented an evil he
could not—and that America must not—fail to resist. Because
of a mixture of fact, prejudice, and innuendo, his controversy
with Catholicism brought him notoriety.

In "The Roman Church" in *Notes on Religion* Chapman
made his diagnosis. Insisting that he had no quarrel with the
claim of this church to bring man to the consciousness of
God, he did have a quarrel with its historical passion for
universal domination, its practice of ecclesiastical government
both in its demand for allegiance to dogma and its denunciation of any difference as heresy. Catholic education was
"the tightest knot of reactionary influence upon the globe,"

and the decision-making power of the Roman Church affected the housemaid in Boston as well as the archbishop in New York City. Like slavery in nineteenth-century America, or like machine politics in twentieth-century America, the church was dedicated to maintaining the status quo. Only the timidity of the American, his preoccupation with making money rather than with thinking, and the silence of the press about the danger of dogmatic religion kept Americans from realizing how insidious was the danger of this religious power to their politics, to education, and even to their domestic life. In addition, Chapman deplored the money paid to a foreign church; the official, ecclesiastical control of political opinion contained in a local parish sermon; and the inflexible attitude of the church about birth control. "I have no desire to extinguish the Catholic faith. . . . The problem of America . . . is to get this subject opened up, upon clear lines, without passion."[10]

Among the reviewers of the book was George Santayana, whose observations made his critique an apology. Chapman to the contrary, Roman Catholicism, Santayana wrote, was not an invention of politicians and sensualists, however many Roman curial origins may have persisted in church administration. Its monolithic power had the virtue of stability amid the instabilities of modern change; it provided both artist and unlettered man with an organic tradition; it was, indeed, a comfort against the American weaknesses of both democracy and Protestantism; and, finally, it was remarkable that Catholicism could flourish at all in passionless and complacent America.[11] The hypersensitivities of ethnic groups in America during the patriotism-charged war years of 1914-18 and the snide allegations of tangled loyalties, dual citizenship, international conspiracy, and treason were part of the background of Chapman's anti-Catholic position of those years. Regrettably, Santayana neglected to correct Chapman's focus of the discussion.

When Chapman published *Letters and Religion* (1924), he omitted his quarrel with the Catholic Church. His non-resistant mood prevailed. By the next year, Chapman had given ear to the domestic mutterings of the KKK. He listened to the international hate-mongers peddling tracts charging that Roman Catholicism was an international conspiracy. Influenced strongly by his brother-in-law William Astor Chanler, he gave credence to the now-discredited *Protocols of the Elders of Zion* which diagrammed an international Jewish conspiracy. And along with the nativists, dismayed at America's immigrant millions in urban ghettos and afraid they were hatching in their foreign languages a Marxist conspiracy, Chapman became obsessed with the danger of subversion in America. He sprayed his vigilante buckshot everywhere.

He argued with Catholic relatives. He wrote anti-Catholic, anti-Semitic verse. He published one sonnet in the *Ku Klux Kourier,* and he thought of hiring a Boston hall for a lecture about the church. He lashed Harvard because it had recently elected a Roman Catholic Fellow of Harvard University. He agitated for his views and won support. Chapman's friend from St. Paul's School and Harvard, Owen Wister, sympathized with and supported him. The *Commonweal,* a Catholic magazine, attacked late in 1924 and in 1925 the views of Chapman and Wister, offered its pages to Chapman for open discussion, and printed letters from its readers (like the non-Catholic architect, Ralph Adams Cram) challenging Chapman's facts. Chapman's disarming reply insisted that he was only trying to defend education in America from Catholic control.[12] Other letter writers answering Chapman reread *Notes on Religion* and did homework on Santayana's earlier rebuttal. Chapman's allegations were scoffed at; but he had achieved what he asserted he wanted: the opening-up of discussion.

Working in Chapman's mind were the literature, the backstairs gossip, and the over-wine-and-cigars talk surrounding the controversial candidacy of Catholic Alfred E. Smith in 1928 for the presidency, a virulent rehearsal for the 1960 Kennedy-Nixon presidential campaign. Chapman refused the *Commonweal* offer and chose the *Forum* magazine for his discussion of the alleged Catholic danger in America. The *Forum* discussion lasted for six months, from March to August, 1925. Drawing upon world history, citing Papal Encyclical, quoting the man-in-the-street, and jubilant at the injured tone of newspaper and magazine protest, Chapman exulted in the opening of the discussion. The argumentative heat generated convinced him that he had an authentic grievance. With the grievance aired, he was sure the cure would follow.[13] Letters originating in almost a dozen states were published. The *Forum,* riding a circulation bounce, promised articles on mixed marriages, the psychology of conversion, and exposure of the KKK. To most people and even to Chapman's family, the controversy smacked of unhealthy bigotry.

Every so often in America under the unnerving pressure of massive tensions, religious, racial, and ethnic viciousness erupts, spewing hate, seeking scapegoats, and exposing the modern merchandising of antique prejudice and vintage superstition. Marriage, divorce, adoption, the practice of contraception or psychiatry, the proscription of a book or a movie, the pressure to remove a magazine from the public files of a school—anything will set off the chain of charge and counter-charge that signals the onset of a social rumble in which phrases are switch-blades and the blacklist works like a blackjack. With Chapman's compulsion to speak out and with his excessive fondness for public fist-shaking and finger-pointing, Chapman agitated a matter too close to the boiling point of blood. The cause was not quixotic. His manner was not irresponsible. Behind his excited remarks was his awareness of the formidable danger to democratic process of any pressure group or lobby, in this case the Roman Catholic Church. The dogmas of a pressure group were in themselves bad; those of a religious pressure group were insidious. Belonging to no pressure group himself, he was able with the clarity of his prose and with the authority of his name to protest; it was, he felt, his inalienable right to do. But one more sidelight on this subject deserves recording.

In 1938 Edmund Wilson printed in *The Triple Thinkers* the best, single, short study of Chapman. He described Chapman's anti-Catholic agitation as one of his most wrong-headed outbursts, for Chapman exaggerated the importance of the church in the United States. When, ten years later, Wilson re-edited and reprinted *The Triple Thinkers*, he made no changes in this opinion. But at this point in his essay he put in an asterisk and appended: "Since this was written, the Catholic Church has become in the United States a formidable pressure group, exercising the retrograde and repressive force that Chapman at that time ascribed to it."[14] To those who agree with Wilson and with Chapman, not out of personal animus but out of principle, perhaps the clue to their reasoning is Chapman's explanation: the fault is not in the church *per se* but in its institutional imperatives flowing out of an undeviating loyalty to dogma, the great deceiver.

II *God in Art*

By many stratagems Chapman prevented his God from being fenced in by institutions, things, and people. Skeptical of almost everything like Montaigne, he was like Montaigne not skeptical of his traffic with the power and energy of mind that men called God. This attitude explains why he was amused at the philosopher's wordy quest for the wordless God. His own intuition of God was best expressed in behavior and in the hieroglyphics of all the arts. God was not the God of history, of reason, of science, of philosophy, and certainly not of psychology or of sociology. Logic could no more describe God than man could describe the taste of a strawberry. "There is a little religious truth in anything that moves us."[15] Emerson's nature that rushed into persons was Chapman's God.[16] Christ needed no intermediary person, no interposing church, no scholar's footnotes. Christ's heroic life "exists as a fiery pathway through the Universe, connecting man with man."[17] The mystic's familiar metaphor of fire, recurrent in Chapman's writing (and more than a metaphor as it concerned his left hand), places his religious views outside the scheme of formal analysis.

To understand his religious thinking we are forced to study his behavior. "Men are reorganized and set in tune by their passing reflections about Christ."[18] Thus, when Chapman (like Walter Lippmann) insisted upon coloring political analysis with the dye of morality; when (like the Reverend John Haynes Holmes) he insisted upon illuminating all social questions with the radiance of Christianity; when (like William James and Henri Bergson) he championed the right to feel one's way to belief; and when (like A. N. Whitehead) he pointed to the spiritual reality behind the minutiae of laboratory science, he was self-defensively adjusting his personal religion to the complications of his civilization and the complexities of new thinking. Civilization was in serious plight of getting drab: it was a "paper-faced . . . iron grey commercial civilization," he had noted in 1897.

To many, his advice was hackneyed, even though common sense often is contained in the commonplace. In the early days of skyscrapers and structural steel he tried to reinvigorate the gospel of The Carpenter. Where he clearly saw the need of relief, he too often urged what was substantially self-reformation. Where limited ends were needed in a crisis, he urged the palliative of idealism. He advocated without hypocrisy, and he acted with altruism a peculiar kind of piety; it was alternately quietistic and militant.

If his seeming inconsistency baffles the casual spectator of his career, the piety Chapman sought was constant. Scattered through his plays and celebrated in children, in Victor, in Minna Timmins, and in the awesome reverence he felt for the arts, especially music, piety undisguised was there. He was stern and strident when he found it masquerading in personal, social, intellectual, or institutional dogma. *Tendency, influence,* and *mystery*—three of his most recurrent words—were his flags of the undefinable. They were like Cupid to Psyche—not to be seen in the betraying light of dogma. Rather were they the "tangibles" of faith—things hoped for and not seen.

Chapman was, in a sense, a statistic in the ambiguous struggle of religion in America to keep pace with other rapid changes in the short but vibrant history of America. The God-centered ideal of Chapman's Huguenot and Puritan ancestors (which he held dear) had long ago lost its force against the attractive comforts of the good life in America. The altruism of the enlightenment had diluted Puritan Christian zeal. Deism and Unitarianism had dwarfed the Great Awakening. The ethics of slavery and Abolitionism had tested both church and believer, and left them both shaken and uncertain. After the Civil War, American industrialization, urbanization, and the diffusion of the financial, capitalistic ethos (bank-certified by Carnegie and Morgan), supported dramatically by science geared to engineering, packaging, and advertising the goods and services of civilian technology (and military technology in a crisis)—these had challenged American religious thinking to re-evaluation. After the Gilded Age, American Protestantism under the spell of Carnegie's Gospel of Wealth awoke late to its neglected social-gospel mission. The cracked social fabric was mended with patchwork missions. Church-going was the spiritless answer to the spiritual vacuum of materialistic, American life with its "acres of diamonds." Pragmatism was all. Chapman, hostile always to church-going, pleaded for a pristine Christianity that would be free of the dogma that kills. He invoked the beneficent effect on the individual of the words and deeds of Christ. He cultivated his private mysticism with its ritual of personal protest.

Meanwhile, any speck on the horizon—Good Government Clubs, Tolstoi, the Boer War, George M. Sheldon's *In His Steps,* the University Settlements, unpublicized philanthropy, civil service reform, Christian Science, the Salvation Army, Felix Adler's Ethical Culture Society, the sacrifices of war, the saint-like lives of altruistic scholars, Abolitionists, educators, penologists, Tagore in America, and especially artists of all kinds—any one of these could set his susceptible nerves a-tingle with the intimations that a religious revival was coming in America, in the world. One wonders what Chapman would have made of the gospel according to *Elmer Gantry*, Norman Vincent Peale, Billy Graham, and Oral Roberts.

Loving "green religion growing" and this sensuous world very much, Chapman strained after knowledge of still another world. In literature he found true intimations of immortality. He himself tried many genres, and he also criticized the literature of half a dozen languages. Words were clues to The Word. Therein lay their charm, their mystery, and their liberating influence, reverberating and persistent, on the certain perfectibility of man and on intellect and character in America.

CHAPTER 6

The Windows of Literature

A LETTER from one of Chapman's friends mentioned that a window had been broken in her home, by whom she did not know. Chapman facetiously and revealingly sent her his sympathies: "I'll tell you my philosophy—that there's only one real joy in life—but fortunately there's likely to be lots of it —the joy of casting at the world the stone of an unknown world."[1] This was 1896, and Chapman was thirty-four. He had published three essays on Michelangelo, Dante, and Shakespeare, and he was writing his memorable essay on Emerson. His own phrase—"the joy of casting at the world the stone of an unknown world"—describes the critical method of the ethically intuitive Chapman.

In his remarks on American, English, French, Greek, Italian, and German literature (and the language and art of biblical writing), his intention as critic of intellect and character in America is persistently and consistently revealed. Why Chapman did not concentrate exclusively on the writing of literary criticism, for which his expert intuition was an incalculable, natural asset, is a minor mystery. The solution probably lies in the fact that he had a horror of specialization because it warped the judgment. Particularism was an intellectual vice. He wanted to put together a critical method which was a synthesis of different methods, including the literary. Besides, he dabbled; but he dabbled seriously, for he loved the literature he criticized. He was, perhaps, victimized also by his facility in various genres, by his suspicion of the narrowly preoccupied literary person, and by his overriding desire to be a historian of manners and morals in a unified sense. "You will find me Plutarch, Thucydides, John Fiske, and Macaulay all in one," he wrote in frolicsome hyperbole in 1897.[2] What is missing from this revealing list of model critics is the name of a systematic literary critic or a far-reaching, deep-diving esthetic critic. With such as these he was impatient; and he made this view clear in his essay "The Aesthetic" in *Learning and Other Essays*. The esthetic, ultimately a mystery, was for Chapman contained in the broad social criticism he hoped to write.

He saw himself as an iconoclast, a window-breaker. Anticipating the effect on Boston of his Emerson essay, he wondered what Boston would look like with all its steeples down. The dogma "that art must come" was merely dogma—a window to be smashed. Pedantry and dilettantism were affectations which issued from dogma banefully cultivated by distinguished critics and prolific journalists. The task he set himself was to assail the dogmas and the critic-dogmatists. His competition was formidable. Besides the established critics—Arnold, Ruskin, Pater, Saintsbury, Sainte-Beuve, Taine, and Lowell—there were others of varying magnitudes and popularity. The quality magazines just before and after the turn of the century offered (among others) the following: J. A. Symonds, Arthur Symons, Augustine Birrell, Georg Brandes, G. B. Shaw, G. K. Chesterton, Henry James, Gilbert Murray, Paul Bourget, Ferdinand Brunetière, W. D. Howells, Barrett Wendell, Gamaliel Bradford, William Brownell, E. C. Stedman, Lewis E. Gates, Irving Babbitt, P. E. More, Hamilton Wright Mabie, William Lyon Phelps, and a host of forgotten reviewer-critics of the *Atlantic Monthly, North American Review, Chap-Book, Harper's, Outlook* and of the English and French reviews which Chapman regularly read.

Chapman collected his own magazine criticism in *Emerson and Other Essays* (1898), which was reviewed with apprecia-tion in the United States and in England. He gave an American writer's name to the book (the only time he was to do that except for his biography of Garrison), but it contained essays on two American writers (Emerson and Whitman). Two were about Italians (Dante and Michelangelo), and three about English writers (Browning, Stevenson, and Shakespeare). The international subject matter was indicative of Chapman's lifelong literary criticism: literature was world literature. (The mixture of Chapman's subject interests is further documented in a list of planned works some of which never came to fruition, others which exist in incomplete manuscript: a drama on John Brown, essays on James Russell Lowell and Carlyle, and a book on Goethe.) Chapman did not have periods of preoccupation with one national literature. He alternated his literary studies, thus defeating boredom. He kept hoping to surprise the mysteries he declared were present in art. In the following pages are collected his observations on the peculiar genius of the half-dozen nations whose writers he judged.

I *American Writers*

Almost all the essays Chapman wrote about American writers may be said to be "bread and butter" letters to men who had inspired him and whose writing had been clear windows opening on vistas of art full of mystery and delight. His criticism is the judgment of a witness, of one who had many religious experiences on his long road to Damascus. Emerson, for instance, had been a family memory. When a boy Chapman had read his works, and he had seen him in his dotage walking in Harvard Yard. Reading in his undergraduate room, long burdened with an unclear definition of himself compared with the clear pictures of his family's solid achievement, worried about his career, attracted to the literary life of Harvard and Boston, thrilled to his innards reading Dante, Michelangelo, and Shakespeare, caught and yet liberated in love with Minna Timmins, graduated into the law, adrift in New York City politics—all these experiences lie behind Chapman's critique of Emerson. Emerson freed him from his doubts, and liberated him to do anything he wanted to do because, in Emerson's richly associative mind (so like Chapman's), everything was related. Emerson was Chapman's Virgil in the American Inferno. What a single man did (or did not do) illuminated the landscape like lightning. And what Emerson wanted for America, Chapman also wanted. Emerson was warrant for what Chapman thought and wrote: his *Nursery*, his political agitation, his independency, his recklessness, and his conviction of his essential ·ightness. "I can't imagine what I should have been if it ıadn't been for Emerson. . . . He let loose something within me which made me in my own eyes as good as anyone else."[3] A painful world of remembered anxieties is contained in the last reminiscence.

The Emerson that Chapman celebrated was the "Yankee Shelley," rhapsodist, lecturer, mystic, eccentric, American scholar, ransacker of the classics and Oriental literature, patriot, reformer, and—above all—radical. To Chapman, Emerson opposed the tyranny of universal suffrage and of conservatism in politics, religion, and business:

> While the radicals of Europe were revolting in 1848 against the abuses of a tyranny whose roots were in feudalism, Emerson, the great radical of America, the arch radical of the world, was revolting against the evils whose roots were in . . . tyranny, and by bringing back the attention of political thinkers to its starting point, the value of human character, he had advanced the political thought of the world by one step. He has pointed out for us in this country to what end our efforts must be bent.[4]

Had not Chapman already discovered his cause—the degradation and obsolescence of the individual in American life—Emerson would have led him to it. But Chapman had already discovered it: it had been revealed to him in family history intricately enmeshed in the symbolic Civil War. The fighting had been the consequence of moral cowardice; pity had aroused the Abolitionists; character had pushed men to the breaking point of humanity. And the war itself had its consequences: it was the beginning of national life in America. In Chapman's time big business (where before there had been big slavery) stepped into the vacuum of moral life to seal young men's lips, to intimidate reform, and to dry out our cultural life. Even as his family had before him fought against the crippling and killing dogmas of slavery, and before that, of religious war, so would Chapman continue to fight. Emerson fortified him. Chapman had his program.

But Emerson had his deficiencies, and they were serious. One was that Emerson insisted on one dogma: the persistent old Calvinistic orthodoxy that the moral law is the absolute truth and that it was self-sufficient for every individual. This position Chapman rejected on two counts. One was that it left out the working of God in the personal affairs of men; and, second, it choked off the intelligence of life supplied by the emotions, by art, and by sexual love. Emerson's Puritan dogmatism and his rejection of the sensuous and sensual freedoms sought by the *Dial* Transcendentalists—"Art was a name to him; music was a name to him; love was a name to him."[5]—were not only remedies worse than the American disease which Emerson had attempted to cure but remedies, moreover, which Chapman would persistently reject. America needed its religious sensibilities reawakened and it certainly needed its artistic life invigorated. God neglected and art despised were to be the basic themes of Chapman's literary criticism.

Around 1900 America, according to Chapman, was still provincial. Puritanism—as Mencken, Van Wyck Brooks, the expatriates, and Eugene O'Neill were to show—was a literary drag on our creativity. Preoccupied by revolution, Civil War, the Western settlement, business aggrandizement, and the dying of village culture, America had depended on European culture for the little self-expression Americans treasured. Lowell, Holmes, and Longfellow had tried to create a national literature, but all they succeeded in doing was to kill Poe and to create Bryant. What was needed was a new American scholar. This was precisely and subtly Chapman's intent in naming his essay published in the *Atlantic Monthly* (1897), "Emerson Sixty Years After"—sixty years after the publication of the American Scholar address in 1837.

If America, about to enter the twentieth century, was not at all fatigued by end-of-century jitters, if America was (as many Americans felt and as Chapman expressed it) the future with a big "F," and if Chapman's brother Henry was right ("Local civilization is dead, and with the twentieth century international civilization begins."),[6] then it was the obvious responsibility of American thinking to lead the world. More than America was promises; the world, too, was promises. Emerson had seen the vision in its patriotic outlines, but Chapman saw it in its cosmopolitan contours.

One other sympathy Chapman shared with Emerson: his dislike for the machinery, associations, or organizations useful if not necessary to combat entrenched wealth, vested interests, and cartelized power. One could be like Jacob Riis, a lone-handed reformer; or one could be like Lincoln Steffens who believed that politics should be fought with politics. Chapman, following his master, chose after his short Good Government Club activity to go it alone. Symbolically, the thirty-six issues of the *Nursery* were largely his own writing. Ultimately he capitulated to pressures greater than a single man could endure. He broke down physically and mentally in 1901. Uncompromising Emersonianism had a high price for Chapman.

But before he took to his bed to rise again a chastened but still militant Emersonian in the twentieth century, Chapman documented in the *Nursery* the endemic flatulence of American thinking and writing. He satirized in "Fifty Years of Harper's Magazine" (June, 1900) the anti-literary contents of the golden anniversary year of its publishing history. John Wanamaker was, he insisted, the real editor of the magazine. Genteel journalism, the object of James L. Ford's attacks in *The Literary Workshop* (1894), was also Chapman's satirical target. In those days Chapman was buoyant, witty, jocular, energetic, and exuberant. Laughter, he insisted, was the true ratsbane for hypocrites. Merely fashionable talk irked him to remonstrance, particularly the literary nervousness expressed on both sides of the Atlantic since 1891 that the end of the nineteenth century portended ominous things. "I don't happen to feel fin-de-siècle in the smallest degree," he wrote in a letter in 1895, "and other people seem to me to have a large share of primeval naturalness about them."

One of the intellectual influences contributing to the ominous sense of the end-of-a-century feeling was a walloping book by Max Nordau (1849-1923) published as *Entartung* in Germany (1891) and as the popular *Degeneration* (1895) in the United States. Chapman was familiar with it as early as 1895. Moreover, Henry Chapman's magazine, the *Bachelor of Arts*, noticed it that year, saying it should be in every college library. That Chapman was influenced by its argument, though he did not acknowledge it, seems decisively clear from his evaluation of Walt Whitman.

Overlooked these many years, *Degeneration* deserves a short summary. It was a view-with-alarm book, the type sporadically popular in literary history. Book I was a forty-four-page record of the symptoms (found in dress, dwellings, opera, concert, art exhibitions, and books); diagnosis (degeneracy, as defined by Morel and Lombroso, indicated in unbounded egoism, impulsiveness, aboulia or lack of will power, inane reverie, mysticism, hysteria, obsessional promulgation of esthetic dogma); etiology (poisoning by increased consumption of alcohol and other narcotics); and resultant fatigue of degeneration. Books II-IV gave the clinical-artistic evidence, the prognosis, and therapeutics for the twentieth century.

Nordau was hopeful that the hysteria would not last; the degenerate would wither away; the aberrations of art would be lost as the new literature rediscovered the old traditions and the established literary forms (*Faust, Divine Comedy, Vanity Fair*). The prescribed therapy was to characterize "the leading degenerates as mentally diseased; unmasking and stigmatizing of their imitators as enemies of society; cautioning the public against the lies of these parasites."[7] The notable "degenerates" on Nordau's list included Baudelaire, Bismarck, Edward Bellamy, Huysmans, Ibsen, Maeterlinck, Nietzsche, Wagner, Whitman, Wilde, and Zola, neo-Catholics, Pre-Raphaelites, and socialists. These were also Chapman's aversions. Shakespeare and Dante were not on Nordau's blacklist—again, Chapman agreeing.

Nordau's judgment of Whitman was that he wrote effusions and outbursts of erotomania; was a crazy American; attracted magnetically to him other deranged minds; was a vagabond, a reprobate rake, effeminate; avoided the difficult in prosody; and wrote his fugitive ideation in formless, tasteless verse. Chapman's treatment of Whitman—published first in the *Chap-Book* (July 15, 1897) and collected in *Emerson and Other Essays*—conceded that Whitman had written a handful of great poems but his faults were those Nordau had attributed to him. Whitman was a tramp, a man of genius in whose work are seen "the elemental parts of a man's mind and the fragments of imperfect education . . . floating and sinking in a sea of insensate egotism and rhapsody, repellent, divine, disgusting, extraordinary." He is an example of aboulia because ideas are not at the bottom of his revolt, which is the revolt of laziness. His poetry has "merely pathological coherence. . . . He is an ego-maniac." He was immoral: "He was neither chaste, nor industrious, nor religious."[8]

His essay on Whitman illuminates Chapman, his method, and his times. Whitman was "a cause" in the 1890's, and Chapman knew it, as his letters of that decade testify. To "attack" Whitman was to hit critical pay dirt. Further, he knew Whitman had been taken up erroneously by the English as a representative example of the American genius. To "attack" the sovereign English literary criticism was to advance American intellectual independence. Chapman insisted that obviously the English were inept in literary criticism. Too hidebound by allegiance to critical rules and therefore too susceptible to the rule-breaker, they had erred in accepting the barbaric

yawp of Whitman as the native voice of America. How very
wrong they were Chapman showed by turning the tables on
Whitman and the English and by mounting an attack on
America.

Simply, America was not as Whitman described it. It was
worse. If an Englishman were to come to America, this is
what he would see:

> He would see an industrious and narrow-minded popula-
> tion, commonplace and monotonous, so uniform that one
> man can hardly be distinguished from another, law-abid-
> ing, timid, and traditional; a community where the in-
> dividual is suppressed by law, custom, and instinct, and in
> which, by consequence, there are few or no great men.
> . . . The culture of this people, its architecture, letters,
> drama, etc., he would find were, of necessity, drawn from
> European models; and its poetry . . . a somewhat feeble
> imitation of English poetry . . . and the newspaper verse
> of the United States is precisely what one would expect
> from a decorous and unimaginative population,—intel-
> ligent, conservative, and uninspired.
>
> (pp. 114-15)

Emerson's criticism of life in America and Nordau's of "degenerates" everywhere had combined in Chapman's mind into
a destructive anti-Whitman, anti-English, and anti-America
essay which opened controversy in which Oscar Lovell Triggs,
E. E. Hale, Jr., Laurence Jerrold, and James Gibbons Huneker
subsequently participated.

Chapman's failure to recognize both the substantial deriva-
tion of Whitman from Chapman's hero, Emerson, and Whitman's equally agonized appraisal of manners and intellect in
America in *Democratic Vistas* suggests both the weakness and
strength of his critical method. Whitman's Civil War experiences should have elicited Chapman's praise. Whitman's
boastful sexuality, a corrective to Emerson's inhibitedness,
was ignored. Chapman early in his critical career was wont
to brag that he did not read about the men he wrote about;
later, in *Dante* and *Lucian* he was more thorough. Indeed,

he teased the texts themselves, directing criticism to literature rather than to history. His criticism would have been more "balanced" had he mediated the claims of contrary scholarship, but he was not interested in that academic "fairness." As a first principle, he suspected the possibility of criticism to unravel the complexity of art. A writing man himself, he intuitively sensed the writer behind the words. Intent upon demonstrating the ingredients for greatness necessary to a sound literature reflecting a sound society grounded in sound individuals, he could see so many deficiencies in Whitman that he had to write him off as a man of letters.

Not Whitman but William Lloyd Garrison was at the center of the American experience. He had nourished the roots of the American myth or legend that was the underground and historic source of our national purpose. Significantly, Chapman first published *William Lloyd Garrison* in 1913, and republished it in 1921. The two dates frame the book around World War I, which Chapman experienced deeply and tried with anguish to understand. *Garrison* was intended in 1913 for young Americans to acquaint them with the historical utility of Abolitionist agitation in awakening the dormant conscience of America and the enrichment of the "Old Legend" of the American Revolution by the "New Legend" of the Civil War. In its reprint edition his new preface expressed the hope, moreover, that adults would read it because the suffering of World War I may have left them "a keener, more religious, and more dramatic understanding of our Anti-Slavery period than we possessed prior to 1914."

Carrying its documentary scholarship gracefully, *Garrison* recorded the painful growth of public opinion and ethical consciousness in ante-bellum America. Chapman asserted that we who have come after are still part of its uncoiling mysterious influence, "supernal, mythological,—typifying the regeneration of a people. The Legend is so vast, and moves at such a pace from beginning to end, that no two minds can agree about its detail. Yet that Legend is at all points illuminated with the inner light of poetry and religion."[9] The victory over slavery had put down (temporarily) the superiority of money over people; it had ended our isolation from Europe; for, being half-free and half-slave, we were so preoccupied by schism that we did not notice the arrest of learning in America. The two men—Garrison, the doer, and Emerson, the sayer of things that nourish conscience and intellect and thereby character—preserved an American idealism almost subverted by the new slavery, the business ethic. By imaginatively reliving the Abolitionist epoch with its decisive war, and fresh from the anxieties of the recent world war, Americans might find renovation in the primal power of both struggles against tyranny and for piety, truth, and love. "Our minds thus dissolve under the grinding analysis of life, and leave behind nothing except God" (278).

Garrison is not a conventionally written history, but it is exciting in its look at history. *Garrison* is not as graceful in either form or style as Chapman's other memoirs of heroes. But it is infused with Chapman's dismay at America's spiritual stumbling and political fumbling. It is also prayerful, especially in the epilogue. It began as a history. It ended as a tract. It also reveals the biblical roots of his historical interpretation.

The history of America was seen under Chapman's mystical light of eternity. His literary criticism, seeking to identify the oneness and integrity of the American character, was no afternoon's pastime lingering over sugared sonnets. The texts Chapman studied were heroic men in motion, moral history in the making, ethical ambiguities, religious paradoxes, and poetic glints and sparks of transcendental fire, of bushes that burned and were not consumed, of things seen through a glass darkly, but, Chapman felt, surely.

These were the major attentions Chapman paid to American writers. His literary table-talk comments, preserved in his letters can be—should be—read conveniently in the early biography of Chapman by M. A. DeWolfe Howe and the more recent critical study by Richard Hovey. They are candid, amusing, and exceedingly quotable. There are many essays, book reviews, and memoirs uncollected from the pages of *Vanity Fair*, the New York *Times Book Review*, the *Yale Review*, and the *Independent* which record his continuous critical interest in the American scene. He had opinions about everything: the folly of prohibition, the waste of razing distinguished buildings in the early stirrings of urban renewal, the decline of portrait painting, the disappearance of the craftsman, the anti-intellectualism of Henry Ford, slovenly writing, the tension between high-brow and low-brow, the League of Nations, the effect of photography on art education, the need for salon culture in America and for the classics in education, the neglect of E. A. Poe, and the loss to America by expatriate writers. He wrote imaginary obituaries of living, well-known contemporaries (the Reverend Percy Stickney Grant, an Episcopalian minister and liberal) and tributes to American saints (Dr. Samuel Gridley Howe, Julia Ward Howe, William James, H. H. Furness, and James L. Ford). Writing the miscellaneous contents of the *Nursery* had given him excellent experience in writing the equally miscellaneous essays of the 1920's. Many of his observations were acute and his diagnoses prophetic. But the five books he published during the 1920's illustrate better how alive to literary matters Chapman was after the war.

The reviewer of *Emerson and Other Essays* in the London *Academy* of August 20, 1898, had hoped, echoing Henry James's hope a few months earlier, that Chapman might be *the* American critic, "the authentic American voice of criticism."[10] At home, *Munsey's* magazine placed "the literary lawyer among the most promising of the literary critics of this country." Critic he would be, except that, on the one hand, he never cultivated the journalistic consideration of American letters and, on the other hand, he was not a systematic student of American literature. The literary West and South went unnoticed; Twain, Harte, Dickinson, Howells, James, Hawthorne, Realism, Naturalism—all received only passing mention. For that matter, he was not a systematizer of the foreign literature he knew so well.

II *English Writers*

To Browning, Kipling, Stevenson, Chesterton, Shaw, and Gilbert Murray, Chapman devoted short essays. About Shakespeare, he wrote several long essays and a book. These men and the critics who wrote about them supplied clues to the genius of English literature and to the pitfalls of a critical method slavishly supplied. All, except Shakespeare, are questioned for their ideas: whether or not they were doctrinal for the times. Only Shakespeare escapes Chapman's characteristic critical practice of making predictions of oblivion. Often a visitor to England, with numerous friends and correspondents in England, Chapman respected the hold English life and letters had on America. He was no Anglophile, no matter how disconsolate he was when he compared English with American conditions. America was not an extension of England; we were merely related. Besides, we could even teach England a thing or two.

To the young Chapman life came crashingly clear in books. He had "revelations." In the seed time of his life Chapman discovered Browning and it was fruitful. Alike in many respects, Chapman embraced Browning for his doctrine; imitated the prosody of his "Cavalier Tunes," as can be noticed in Chapman's *Songs and Poems* (1919); and mulled over Browning's burning lines about self, music, reason, truth, love, and God. It is not hard to imagine what Browning's autobiographical lines in "Pauline" meant to Chapman:

> but I have never doubted:
> So as I grew, I rudely shaped my life
> To my immediate wants; yet strong beneath
> Was a vague sense of power though folded up—
> A sense that though those shades and times were past,
> Their spirit dwelt in men, with them should rule.

. . . .

For music (which is earnest of a heaven,
Seeing we have emotions strange by it,
Not else to be revealed,) is like a voice,
A low voice calling fancy, as a friend,
To the green woods in the gay summer time.

．　．　．　．　／　．　．　．　．　．　．

What is that I hunger for but God?

．　．　．　．　．　．　．　．　．　．　．

O reason's pedantry, life's rule prescribed!

．　．　．　．　．　．　．　．　．　．　．

Sun-treader, I believe in God and truth and love. . . .

All art, dexterity, virtuosity, and scholarship in painters, musicians, theologians, scientists, and teachers—and in men and women in love—ended in a mystery to Browning. And they did to Chapman. Browning's celebration of art and love were antidotes to Emerson's anemia. His gallery of individuals were countervailing inspiration to the "isms" and "ologies", the scientism and mass philanthropies, of the Victorian period —abstractions which obliterated the individual. Browning was an aristophile and an optimistic Christian; so was Chapman— and America needed both the love of the best and a living sense of the regenerative mystery of God. To read Browning was better than reading Carlyle, and, in some respects, better than reading Emerson. To know his poetry "becomes a liberal education," which was what America needed.[11]

Kipling, however, was not what America, or the world, needed. Chapman could praise the Kipling who described India with the magic of an artist, but he could only be dismayed and fearful of the Kipling who, after a visit to South Africa, had discovered imperialism. This idea made his work rubbish, made him rich by supplying a journalistic market for his wares, and turned him into a class poet of race prejudice: "A poet must think he is the voice of humanity. . . . A man who schedules himself as the poet of Anglo-

Saxondom is a *littérateur*. He is a class poet. We cannot accept this race prejudice. There is nothing in it."[12]

Just as Chapman went his own way in evaluating Browning (against the grain of the numerous and adulatory Browning clubs of the era), so he went his independent way in measuring Kipling. Charles Eliot Norton and Paul Elmer More could praise Kipling in the popular magazines; Chapman could not. Art could not redeem what Chapman believed were basically noxious ideas. America—involved in the Spanish-American War and just then stepping into a power position in international politics—that Chapman insisted did not then know the difference between Cecil Rhodes and David Livingstone could well do without Kipling's cant.

Chapman's interest in and knowledge of the techniques and history of literature were utilized appreciatively in all his literary estimates, but he concentrated his critical energies on the "doctrine" of the man under scrutiny, the ideas which made the writer doctrinal to man's best hopes for man. Sometimes these ideas revealed in a flash a nation; other times, only a sign of good or bad times ahead. In Robert Louis Stevenson's case, his theories and practice of writing were fundamentally injurious, especially since he was so popular. When Stevenson sacrificed speaking in his own voice for the "effete, backward-looking" voices of archaic and dead styles—albeit cleverly done—this act of insincerity by an artist degraded both art and the artist. It followed that his work was "whipped up literary froth." He was an eclectic who saw himself self-consciously as "an artist" and his writing as "performances." In such Nordauist terms did Chapman characterize the Stevenson Americans read, while thinking they were reading "literature." It was a sign of the times (and a good one) that America hungered for literature; but America ought to know that whipped up literary froth was not precisely the nourishing food it needed.[13] For the same Nordauist reasons, and in language recalling Nordau's attack on Oscar Wilde and the Pre-Raphaelites, Chapman expressed his dislike for G. K. Chesterton and G. B. Shaw in his essay "Jesters" in

Learning and Other Essays. They shared in common "a loss of delicacy. They are crude: they are all edge. They are, indeed, a little vulgar" (152). In these judgments Chapman's Puritanism lapsed into the puritanical.

III *Victorianized Greek*

In Chapman's view, the practice of literary criticism was a very dubious enterprise. Obviously, when a writer exhibited himself preciously in a work, or when his baneful ideas were hardly worth the art, his work was bad for readers. A critic was useful when he pointed out these faults. But when critics, translators, or academic scholars deflected the right understanding of Greek literature (or Shakespeare), it was a worse situation. They were doing positive evil not only to the works themselves but to generations of schoolboys who studied their perverse pronouncements. Chapman's scepticism of the value of literary criticism appears to beg the question of Chapman's own criticism. If, to Chapman, criticism was in the first place impotent to explain art, then both he and the critics were in a root-and-branch sense quite dispensable. But critics criticized; they could not be ignored. Making the best of a bad situation, it was important, therefore, to Chapman to diminish the dissemination of positively bad criticism. The historical criticism of the nineteenth century was a case in point.

English scholarship on Greek literature was dominated in the late nineteenth century by two Englishmen, Benjamin Jowett (died 1893) and Gilbert Murray (alive and famous when Chapman argued against his influence). English cultural imperialists, they Victorianized the Greeks. Murray especially, supported by the sickly estheticism of Pater and Swinburne, had translated sturdy Greek literature into a "limp Grecism." Citing hemistich and strophe of Murray's translations, Chapman showed how Murray had Anglicized, moralized, sentimentalized—in short, perverted—the Greek genius. For Murray to introduce modern theological ideas into Greek texts and to splash a sentimentalized Christian

God all over their pages were unconscionable errors. "The reader becomes so concerned about Mr. Murray's religious obsessions that he forgets the Greek altogether. . . ."[14] Chapman insisted that the Greek genius was different from the English genius. Arnold's sweetness and light and Murray's sweetness and pathos better explained the sorry condition of intellectual England than they defined the intrinsic attributes of Greek civilization. A reader might be brought up short by this line taken by Chapman. After all, was not Chapman emotionally and intellectually compelled to see the world as religious event? He was. But he was also restrained. He could not honestly claim Greek literature as a Christian document. The fact was that Greek art *was* great. Another fact was that biblical literature was greater. With these facts in view, Chapman did not have to raise Olympus over Zion, its literature over the Testaments, and surely not its gods over God. It was Puritan Milton's choice all over again. And Chapman chose as Milton did. Paradise regained was worth it.

IV *Shakespeare*

To rescue not only Greek literature but also Shakespeare from the pedants with the burglar tools and blackjacks was another of Chapman's lifelong, self-imposed, happy tasks:

There is a history of criticism which will go on forever, and Shakespeare's relation to it is indubitably very important. But Shakespeare's direct influence upon the great body of men who know nothing about this whole branch of learning is what makes him Shakespeare. The Gospels are not encrusted in theology, because biblical criticism has never adhered to the New Testament. So literary and dramatic criticism do not stick to Shakespeare. There is some sort of *vis major* behind the Gospels, and there is a *vis major* behind much of Shakespeare which nothing touches. This power draws and fascinates the scholar; it chains him to his desk and to his thesis; it does not, as a rule, liberate his intellect. The scholar whose imagination is alive is a rarity. Indeed, scholarship proverbially kills the imagination; and therefore in striving to find what is our own in Shakespeare—who is the greatest storehouse of imagination in the world—we should be indifferent to scholarship. Everyone of us has a personal share in this wealth, a special relation to this mountainous loadstone of attracting intellect. No matter what we find, we cannot carry it away, nor can we ever force anyone else to perceive and value our discovery exactly as we do.[15]

Chapman slipped through the dense underwater growth of Shakespeare criticism with the skill and touch of an electric eel. He was blithely secure in his possession—never fixed, always imaginatively liberating—of Shakespeare. It had been Shakespeare that his own father always read; it was Shakespeare that Chapman's intellectual father Emerson had chosen as representative of mankind's poets. Indeed, Emerson to Chapman was Shakespeare's younger brother. As for Chapman himself, it was Shakespeare's diction and stagecraft that he imitated in his own poems and plays; it was Shakespeare's plays he read to children on his lawn or in settlement houses; it was for Shakespeare that he helped Walter Hampden to stage Shakespeare's plays; it was the study of Shakespeare that was the starting place of "true education."[16]

Chapman coaxed readers away from the steadily proliferating Shakespeare criticism and back to the texts, away from the second-hand experiences of the critics to the first-hand subjective, psychological, literary and magical experience of the reader himself. That twentieth-century Shakespeare criticism was in strong revolt against nineteenth-century Romantic criticism (the adventure of the soul among masterpieces) Chapman does not stop to debate. To him, all criticism tended to make all literature a collection for a wax museum.

To Chapman, Shakespeare's plays were only comprehensible if one imagined how vibrant manners and customs were in Elizabethan days. "We in America, with our formal manners, our bloodless complexions, our perpetual decorum and self-suppression, are about as much in sympathy with the real element of Shakespeare's plays as a Baptist parson is with a fox hunt."[17] As noted earlier in Chapman's criticism of Whitman's critics, literary criticism illuminated character and manners in America. Reading Shakespeare did not lead back to the aridities of historical scholarship but forward into an understanding of current American life. He was to be read only for the pleasure that permits contact with his large, impersonal mind—with "its fondness for the dramatic beauties of the old religion"—but he was to influence us in myriad ways. "He is by far the most popular poet in the world," Chapman wrote in *Greek Genius*, "and teaches metaphysics to millions who do not know they are learning, but find in him merely a fellow-being who loves and understands them."

When we place Chapman's superlative praise of Shakespeare next to Emerson's, all the latter's points are there, but amplified and filtered through Chapman's acute sensibilities and pungent phrase-making. And there is more. Chapman insisted he was rescuing Shakespeare the artist from the landslide of accumulated criticism that had almost buried him. By insisting on isolating the man and his art as he is revealed in his plays and poems, Chapman was saying: "You, American readers, who are avid for learning, don't be scared off by the ponderous critics. Shakespeare was but a man. You are also a man. Open his books. Open your eyes. Read. You will understand. Self-reliance is all. Mountain answers to mountain, and deep unto deep. Come, make the step. Here are the steps I took. This is what I saw. What do you see? What you see and take away will not be another's. It will be yours. Come." The *Complete Shakespeare* could be left, along with the Gideon Bible, in the hotel rooms of America, and America would be the better for it.

V   *Balzac*

The unaligned, free readers of the world might reasonably get together someday to celebrate Chapman's persistent efforts to rescue the great writers of the world from the little critics who build Berlin walls around their captive subjects. Toward Balzac Chapman felt the same sense of protectiveness he showed for the correct translations of Greek plays and the correct view of Shakespeare. In "Balzac," an essay in *Greek Genius*, Chapman evinces a first-hand knowledge of French literature with disarming casualness. The effect (certainly intended by Chapman) is to send the reader not to other critics but back to the texts of the *Comédie Humaine*. What the reader would find there was a commendable literary treatment of life antidotal to the Naturalism that followed Balzac—a wrong road taken, insisted Chapman. For Chapman was not easily flexible in his literary tastes; they had been set early, and new movements and new writers did not compel his attention. He seemed more disposed to protect the old writers from the new critics.

Chapman's essay rescued Balzac from the rule-bound, pure genre-bound French Academy and from the commissar critic, Émile Faguet. In "Balzac," Chapman is a brilliant amateur, a formidably sensitive reader, a meritorious comparative critic, and a deft antagonist of parochial literary judgments. The academic tags pinned on Balzac by Academy-minded critics and the charges that he confused the genres, wrote clumsily, had no esthetic, and had a low view of human nature proved only one thing: France "has constantly produced men who were too great to be understood by the Academy. . . . Balzac seems to be like Rembrandt and Shakespeare in that he is always Balzac, and yet he never does the same thing twice. . . . Balzac, like Dante, suffers from a lack of humour; but one feels the absolute benevolence of Balzac, whereas we know that Dante's benevolence is cut into by political hatreds and by petty theological dogmas."[18]

What made Chapman wince at the low view of human nature in Naturalistic writing and caused him to reject it as "truth" he declared in "Balzac": "I am not willing to give my painful attention to reading a novel if the book is only a restatement of life's injustices and incongruities, a mere attack on the incomprehensibility of the universe. I must have something that confirms the faith in me which the real world so constantly baffles. This is what great works of art do for us" (273). That the world and existence were absurd—the plaint of existential fiction of the mid-twentieth century—was untenable to Chapman.

Art can, does, and must give order and the meaning of order to the faulty sense of haphazardness and inconsequence we frequently, almost daily, experience outside of art. To Chapman, this function was the supreme one. It validates its creation and our human interest in its fictional, fabricated composition. (Chapman's position is similar to that of Joseph Wood Krutch in *Experience and Art*, 1932, and recently reprinted.) It is not an old fogey's position. It is an intellectually respectable position. Chapman provided a revealing sidelight on his position.

In a curious essay, "La Vie Parisienne," immediately following "Balzac" in *Greek Genius*, Chapman was ostensibly commenting on the negative effect on American life of expatriates. They should stay home and better things here. He was also fussily nervous about the effect of the entrenched immoralities in Europe on American visitors. He had read Henry James, William Dean Howells, and Edith Wharton; and he had noticed that:

> The novelists have given us pictures of the climbing American girl—pictures perhaps too dark, yet true in the main. They show that by the mere instinct of climbing, or the mere passion for excitement, a certain type of American woman finds herself in Paris. These novels often come from the hands of the women themselves, and show a great mastery over one side of the subject. They depict with unchristian gusto the moral degeneration of the characters. They seem to be punishing the children of their own imaginations, as if the creatures were their personal enemies. The general tendency of social fiction has of late years been towards this sort of cruelty. . . .
>
> (293-94)

What Chapman seems to have discovered is the mechanism and mechanics of self-hate. He saw it as a self-destructive, inverted love, and a perverse ordering of experience. It was a state of mind. Art through order, right order, could free people from and not subjugate them to hateful, self-punitive impulses. As great as Chapman felt Zola was, Zola's naturalistic fiction reinforced the self-destructive, not the creative, in men. Love not hate and more life not suicide were the instruments and goal of living. The artistic fecundity of Balzac, Shakespeare, Browning, and Emerson proved to Chapman that art divines unself-consciously the spiritual truths of the universe. It kinetically demonstrates the potential wholesome force of literature to bring man to his own majestic self-knowledge.

VI *The Greek Genius*

Greek literature—a window which looked two ways, out on the past and in on the present—was useful on both accounts. Hellenism served as contrasting complement to Hebraism. Concern with one served as relief from the other. Chapman critically played one against the other.

Harvard did not make Chapman into a classicist. While a prep boy he had purchased a 1503 Greek-text *Lucian* because he wanted to own a folio Aldus. At Harvard, he tutored a fellow student in Greek. He never forgot George Herbert Palmer's classroom reading of Palmer's translations of the *Odyssey*. In 1910 he fashioned a play with an American theme, *The Treason and Death of Benedict Arnold,* into a "play for a Greek theater." He did homework in Greek with his son Conrad and salvaged from the sweet, parental task his published paraphrases, *Homeric Scenes* (1914). His *Cupid and Psyche* was staged at the Yale Art School in 1916. *Romulus and Remus* (1916), a grim and wooden children's play, is, for all its apparent didacticism, a look into Chapman's own pain-streaked experience. The evidence is abundant that he subdued the classics to his own possession. What was easy for him was easy for others. His advice in the essay "Greek as a Pleasure" in *Memories and Milestones* (1915) was that to learn Greek was easy so long as one read Greek literature as literature and not as a source book for Greek paradigms.

As with Balzac and Shakespeare, Greek literature had to be protected against its academic misrepresentation. It was in the public domain, an open preserve. It could not be pre-empted by specialist-scholars, trained in Teutonic scientific scholarship or intent upon Christianizing it. They were, simply, marauders or holy pirates. Their good intentions—the pursuit of knowledge, missionary zeal—were out of all proportion to the gross social error and grievous intellectual harm they did in closing off access to the experiencing of Greek literature by the general reader. The Greek genius must be seen for what it was *to the Greeks,* not for what some thesis-ridden specialists saw through the distortions of their spectacles. To force the exquisite beauty of a Greek myth, play, frieze, lyric, pagan religious mystery cult, choric dance, or philosophic dialogue to a dry-as-dust disquisition on psychology, nature-myth tension, or Anglican theological orthodoxy was to commit the cardinal deadly sin of pride. Chapman with the forthrightness of a child speaking truth was determined to tell the world that those dynastic emperors and nobles of German and English scholarship really did not have any clothes on. In his "Euripides and Greek Genius," in which he analyzed the *Alcestis* and the *Bacchantes* as plays and not as tracts, cited the "limp Grecism" of English translations, and contradicted the misleading scholarly annotations accompanying those texts, Chapman hoped to save "the ingenuous stripling from Oshkosh whose father has saved money to send him to college in New Haven" from learning those "grotesque ideas."

All was not offense in this urbane, sophisticated, sarcastic, witty, ironical, richly allusive, and well-tempered essay. Much was defense and lucid analysis. Chapman led the reader back to the texts themselves, to the consideration of the plays as plays (they were antique marble to our modern sandstone); they were fictions, and their effects, imaginative; they were like opera, and their effects, operatic; they were musical drama, whose necessary music was, unfortunately, lost; they were like Molière's plays in their precise and clever manipulations of stage conventions; they were not metaphysical systems and, therefore, not like Milton's plays; they helped us to understand the social life of Athens, the laughter of Aristophanes, the Parthenon, the clubroom atmosphere of a Platonic dialogue, and the several imperishable idiosyncrasies of the Mediterranean mind. For a reader desiring initiation into the dynamics of Chapman's literary criticism, this essay in *Greek Genius* may well be a good place to begin. Reading the classics thereafter, and Greek drama in particular, is bound to be more exciting. Literary criticism that does this is good criticism.

All his life Chapman kept up what he modestly called his scraps and rags of Greek. Filled with grief of Victor's death, Chapman locked himself in and read Plato for ten days. Another time, deep in the emotionalism of scrutinizing Scripture, he found relaxation in paraphrasing Sophocles's *Philoctetes* and Euripides' *Medea*, publishing them in *Two Greek Plays* (1928), and *The Antigone of Sophocles* the next year. He read the *Philoctetes* and *Medea* at two Bromley lectures at Yale. Ultimately, he had to renounce the Greeks for almost the same reason he could not abide Naturalism in fiction. In his "Memoranda" to *Antigone* he confessed:

> The trouble I find with most Greek plays is that they appeal to a sentiment to which I cannot honestly respond, namely to the enjoyment of horror—the horror of ancestral crimes, the horror of marrying one's mother or of being passionately loved by one's stepmother; to the horror of the somewhat monotonous idea that a grisly fate is creeping toward the chief character, and that to express this idea vividly is the highest function of dramatic art. I even go so far as to believe that the Greek enjoyment of these things was artificial, overrefined, and in a sense the enjoyment of aesthetes.

(67)

Chapman was intellectually indomitable. Neither criticism
nor literature was an exercise in anthropology, in Freudianism,
or in technique that preened itself self-consciously and distracted the reader. Moreover, literature could not induce in
him ideas of futility, decadence, pessimism, and absurdity. If
it did or tried to, he suspected it. Chapman's biography
indicates how close to the bone those words described his
contest for wholeness and wholesomeness. His literary
criticism was a window on his mind. The source of his
indomitable courage is clear. After all, there was nothing
decadent, futile, pessimistic, or absurd about Christ.

Chapman's last stand as an independent classicist was in
Lucian, Plato and Greek Morals (1931). When he was about
fifteen he had purchased the folio Aldus *Lucian;* at seventy
he published a book on Lucian. In it he was Emerson's bulldog
and Nordau's watchdog. It was his *Paradise Regained*; in it
he rejected the Greek tradition for the Puritan conscience. It
is virtually a summary of the method and content of his
criticism. Just as he had set off Garrison against Emerson, so
he set off Lucian against Plato—to the credit of Lucian.

In Chapman's exposition, Lucian was a Romanized man of
intellect with a personality as gay as that of Offenbach or
Anatole France. He was a literary scavenger and wit, artist,
gentleman, and man of the world. Fundamentally benevolent,
he used his irony (*the* secret of the Hellenic intellect) as a
sceptical recorder of the decadent Greek world, revealing it
for what it was—provincial, benighted by race tradition and
artistic and metaphysical conservatism. To comprehend
Lucian, Chapman asserted, was to understand the scepticism
of the Renaissance, the age of Louis XIV, the prissiness of the
Victorian Period, the lure of Paris to American expatriates,
"the vaporings of Jung and Freud," and the baneful influence
of Proust. He relished Lucian because he attacked quacks,
scholars, pimps, decadent dramatists, cunning dialecticians,
professional philosophers, and homosexuals—including Plato.
Lucian, the non-Hellene whose ethical passion had "the heat

of religion," was "the apostle of common sense," the man of courage of conscience and conduct. Conscience in conduct would always be a better guide to purposeful living than the intellectual sophistry of Greek intellectualism.

In considering Plato, Chapman judged Plato according to every criterion that Emerson had used in his *Representative Men,* and added a few more. Plato was a writer of fairy tales; his dialogues were drawing-room diversions, essays in romantic speculations; his failure to understand Socrates' death (to Chapman, a clear instance of the triumph of conscience over conduct, a triumph of what the antislavery people called the Higher Law) indicated how far removed from life and how lost in his world of art Plato was. Yet Plato was an influence. Some influences were for the bad—Plato's; some for the good —Lucian's. The bad were degenerative, especially so when they were allied with sexual abnormalities.

In Chapter IV, "Lucian Attacks Pederasty," Chapman thanked Lucian for handing him "a small key to a very large and vague problem" of why was it that Plato, and consequently so much Attic literature, affected Chapman as play, as bits disengaged from life, as touched with decadence. Lucian did not mince words. He named Plato as a pederast. The effect on Chapman was that Plato, the *Symposium,* the abnormal love ethic of homosexual and lesbian—in short, the abnormality of the Attic mind—all came clear. Lucian had been an honest man, and honesty was more enduring than platonic preciosity. It was strange and regrettable that fame, history, and scholarship had so misrepresented both Plato and Lucian. The reasonable remedy for this error was to speak out; name names; cite verse, page, and book; and agitate the question. Chapman's advice was not to ban Plato, but for teachers to tell the truth to students. *Lucian, Plato and Greek Morals* was a sturdy piece of practical literary agitation which insisted on the thesis that sexual love was a cause of character and conduct, and it had its consequences in the art of a civilization. The stone of common sense was a good one to hurl through the windows of Transcendentalists and pundits. It was particular fun when the stone was Lucian's and the house, Plato's.

VII *Italian Writers*

The year after his marriage to half-Italian Minna Timmins, whose Milanese Italian he soon mastered and with whom he had read Dante in their hectic courting days, Chapman published his first essay in the *Atlantic Monthly,* "The Fourth Canto of the Inferno" (November, 1890). In 1927, thirty-seven years after his first published essay on Dante, he published an influential book about Dante. The only other essay restricted to an Italian writer was "Michael Angelo's Sonnets," published in his brother's *Bachelor of Arts* (June, 1895) and collected in *Emerson and Other Essays,* along with the paraphrase of Canto 4 of the *Inferno.*

The clues to Chapman's interest in Italian literature go beyond his biography. Michelangelo and Dante are counterpoints, like Emerson and Garrison, like Lucian and Plato. Chapman's critical method exploited contrast and comparison. His literary men were *exempla,* moral instances of intellects of the world, visibly monumental in the vistas of civilized history, living forces despite the scholarly débris that threatened to bury them; and, as potential influences for emergent culture in America, they carried with them also immense promises of the good life for men everywhere. "The use of great men," Chapman said in *A Glance Toward Shakespeare,* "is to bind the world together."

Michelangelo, for instance, was a *maestro.* The craft of his sonnets suggests his plastic art; the virtuosity of his several arts, the sonnets. These elements were beyond the power of literary criticism to define. What criticism might do—tangentially, indirectly, obliquely, suggestively, never dogmatically, and, least of all, cocksurely—was to indicate the depths of soul, the caverns of mind, the resources of character, and the dynamics of ideas in tradition as they decipher the unity of heaven and earth, of God and man. Michelangelo's poems "are a window which looks in upon the most extraordinary nature of modern times,—a nature whose susceptibility to impressions of form through the eye allies it to classical times; a nature which on the emotional side belongs to our own day."[19] Past and present are bound together by the intelligence supplied by taste in the arts. The modernity in his sonnets is the love expurgated of bestiality and infiltrated with spirituality, human reverence, piety—indeed, Protestant Christianity:

> There is a certain note of the spirit which, when we hear it, we perfectly recognize as a part of ourselves. What we recognize is, in fact, the Protestantism which swept over Europe during the century of Michael Angelo's existence; which was conquered, but not extinguished, in Latin Europe; and a part of which survives in ourselves. If one wishes to feel the power of Savonarola, one may do so in these sonnets. We had connected Michael Angelo with the Renaissance, but we are here face to face with the Reformation. We cannot help being a little surprised at this. We cannot help being surprised at finding how well we know this man.
>
> (161)

Chapman's ability to dive deep for an idea, jolting the reader with the freshness of his find, is here made explicit. We may have given the impression that Chapman's criticism was a tiring and familiar evangelicalism. The import of the preceding quotation should preclude such an interpretation. That Protestantism was an "idea" that qualified the history of the Western world is central to Chapman's thought.

Chapman, the novice translator—perhaps, paraphraser—of Dante in 1890 was, in 1927, the date of *Dante,* a far-ranging and practiced critic and a longtime member of the Dante Society of Cambridge, Massachusetts. Chapman on Dante deserves a monograph in itself, and only some high points will be touched on.

Chapman contrasted Shakespeare and Dante, finding them opposites of poetic temperament. Humorless, didactic, and egoistic, Dante nevertheless triumphed as a poet over these disabilities. The architectonics of his poetry; the unremitting sense of mission and thought; the persistent turning of his experience into self-expression; the penitential tone of the *Comedy* revealing a man singed by politics and love, isolated by learning, and saved by religion; the almost identifiably Protestant impulse in Dante to settle the religious question for himself, taking as much or as little of the church's teaching as he saw fit—these earned Chapman's appreciation of Dante as a poet, his disparagement as a character, and his amazed wonder about him as a force.

Dante was full of learning and free of footnotes, an instance itself of what Chapman was after: an almost suffocated Dante excavated from the rubble of pedantic scholarship, arrogant doctoral looters, and well-intentioned but foolish academicians:

> The arrogance with which we sit down to sum up the Past, and advise our young Ph.D.'s—who have never written a couplet—to write essays about the influence of Shenstone on Wordsworth, is perhaps a sign that the epoch is drawing to a close. The absurdity of it is revealed in its dissolution. . . . We have been endeavoring to express the fluid universe of man's emotions in terms and symbols drawn from the study of physical science; and in the meantime we have all but forgotten the languages of Art, Poetry, and Religion which alone can express the passion for truth with which we burn.
>
> (98-99)

About four pages of *Dante* which included these words were reprinted with the title "Dante and Modern Criticism" and without comment in the "General Articles" section of the *New Republic* of June 8, 1927. The selection was probably put there at the suggestion of Edmund Wilson, who had reviewed *Dante* in that magazine less than a month before (May 18, 1927) and who had urged that Chapman's "eloquent protest at the end against the modern scientific criticism of literature deserves general attention." Book reviews of *Dante* by Charles A. Dinsmore, Christian Gauss, and Charles H. Grandgent—all distinguished Dante scholars—sympathetically re-echoed this point. Two years later T. S. Eliot's essay on Dante (collected in his *Selected Essays, 1917-1932*) had many coincidental quotations, many of Chapman's points, and seems, further, to answer Chapman's objections and faults. Also, Chapman seems to be introducing to the general reader for whom he wrote his books Benedetto Croce's approach to understanding Dante.[20] In turn, Chapman's criticism influenced Papini's criticism of Dante.[21]

Dante, too, had to be saved from the academicians and for the readers. Chapman's attention to the texts has won support. In recent years graduate education in the United States has been trying to throw off the desiccating influence of "scientific" literary scholarship. The popularity, until recently, of the New Criticism in colleges and magazines is also connected with Chapman's plea for his brand of humanistic literary criticism. The fact that the New Criticism in its turn developed its critical excesses and preciosities and lost sight of the text, as did the scientific scholarship Chapman had so consistently and frequently tried to disestablish with satirical skill, is amply documented in current critical discussions, particularly by René Wellek.

Any estimate of Chapman as a translator must be made as if one were walking with spiked shoes on eggs, for the amateurs in this matter are ever at war with the scholars. Over the years Chapman translated a few of Michelangelo's sonnets, Hector's farewell and the wrath of Achilles from the *Iliad*, some of *The Divine Comedy*, and the *Antigone* and the *Philoctetes* of Sophocles, and the *Medea* of Euripides. In all cases he was careful to publish his position: he convivially saluted the fraternity of amateurs over the ages and warned off the vulture pedants who lay in wait for such naïvely self-sacrificing prey as Chapman. His anti-pedanticism was a joy to him, a relish he shared with Lucian and Rabelais:

"Blessings and farewell," he wrote in his Memoranda to *Two Greek Plays* (1928), "to all the camp followers and sumpter mules of learning. . . . For the earthworms of scholarship are destined to go on forever fertilizing the soil by going up and down in it."

What emerges from Chapman's personal preoccupation with literature of many tongues is the ever-presentness of literature itself. He issues invitations to readers (young, impressionable readers hopefully on their way to enjoying the books of the world) to tackle the thesaurus of the Western world with freeborn ingenuity. He cautions against the apparatus of graduate schools, the pontifications of textual archaeologists, and the "Don't Tread on Me" legend imprinted on covers of learned books that do thought and learning a huge disservice. They frighten off the readers. Reading in Chapman can be a liberating experience in the library or in the easy chair at home. He is rich in this effect upon readers. In inducing this effect upon others Chapman reproduces the effect Emerson had on him. Both Emerson and Chapman have this same liberating effect on readers today. It is an effect which Theodore Baird, reviewing Barzun's *Chapman*, tried to catch when he described Chapman's force as "impertinent" and some of his ideas as "heady doctrine to teach the young." Chapman was not only a writer; he also valiantly protected literature from becoming a palimpsest of scholars.

VIII   *Goethe*

The unfinished and unpublished literary criticism of John Jay Chapman includes short essays on Tolstoy, Carlyle, The Book of Job, Henry Adams, and a book-length study of Goethe. He may have tried to probe the "German Genius" (as he tried to do to the Greek Genius through Euripides and Plato; the English Genius through Shakespeare and Browning; the American Genius through Emerson, Garrison, Whitman, and various memoirs) in *Deutschland über Alles,* in the remarks on German scholars widely scattered in his numerous writings, and particularly in his unpublished manuscript *Goethe,* now in the Houghton Library, Harvard. A distinguished Goethe scholar, Dr. Victor Lange, has remarked in correspondence that this manuscript throws more light on Chapman than it does on Goethe, but this statement is not necessarily a critical veto.

In his study of Goethe Chapman tried to extricate the artist and the man from the mass of adulation that obscures him. Goethe was a particular kind of egoist, different from Shakespeare and from Dante. Whereas Shakespeare was the unconscious artist and Dante the strong-called conscious artist subduing even church doctrine to his own personal and poetic purpose, Goethe, the real Goethe, not the Goethe mythicized by nativist German scholarship, was a good deal less than the literary Colossus of the Western world. He was, in fact, a kind of playboy of the Western world. It was not Goethe's profligacy that Chapman objected to; it was not Goethe's using his private life for literary copy; rather it was Goethe's superimposed rationalized explanation: that he was experimenting with life for his self-improvement and self-education. While writing the book, Chapman said in a letter:

> I think Goethe drifted into one thing after another as every one does. . . . As to self-improvement and self-education, it is a trap, an illusion, a pleasing idiocy, a brain-softening indulgency. . . . Now Goethe was a great amateur and never quite toed the mark—except as above universally acknowledged in small poems and parts of Faust, and he had the Teutonic passion for self-improvement. . . .
>
> (Howe, 445-56)

Goethe was to be explained as a victim of a manufactured dogma—namely, that there is some such thing as self-will, that a man can remake himself, and that other people existed for the perfection of his self. Such a dogma disproportionately raised mind over emotions which, thwarted, strike back against the mind. Chapman's criticism showed the

dynamics of neuroticism as they illuminated the *Ur-Faust,*
Faust, his *Discourses,* and the between-the-lines meanings of
Goethe's letters and love affairs. Without spying, peeping, and
wire-tapping, Chapman seems able to hand us, with a sense
of immediacy, the writer self-revealed in his works. We are
somewhat taken aback that we had not noticed the matter
before. This experience explains, perhaps, why critic-reviewers
of Chapman's books frequently flung names at him such as
"crank" and "debunker". They reacted with strong feelings
against his acute intuitions of the man behind the writings,
the personality and character behind the fame, and the moot
sources of energy that created literary libraries by the world's
great writers.

To Chapman, the world's greatest book was the Bible, and
its greatest mind was Jesus. Such statements would have been
the burden of a book by Chapman on the Bible as literature.
He approximated these statements in *Letters and Religion*
and *Notes on Religion* and in his comments preserved in
letters. The world was a reflection of God; everything in the
world was malleable in the hands of God. Even science
sought God fumblingly with its calipers, he said in "Climate"
in *Learning and Other Essays.* In the same collection in the
essay "The Comic," he observed, thinking of Aristophanes:
"There is a kind of laughter that makes the whole universe
throb. It has in it the immediate flash of the power of God.
We can no more understand it than we can understand other
religious truth" (169).

It must be insisted that such criticism is not the thin
obscurantism of Christian apologetics. The most recurrent
images in Chapman's writing—flashes, lightning, sparks—belong to the worldwide mystic's image of fire that burns but
does not consume. Chapman's twenty-five published books
are formulations of his certitude of a divine order in the
world. It was an order more fluid than the theologian's dogma,
the scientist's fact, the philosopher's abstraction, the pedant's
shibboleth, the censor's no-trespass sign, or the prosecutor's
charge of heresy, non-conformity, or independence. They

were all wall-builders, all fence makers who arrested the flux of things. All things bore a message: "There is a little religious truth in anything that moves us. Every art is full of it. The arts are sounding boards that stand behind us as we listen; shade trees that bend above us as we look. They are reverberators and enlarge our naked powers."[22]

Chapman used literary criticism in at least six ways. He de-emphasized the supremacy of critics over the works they set out to elucidate; restored the importance of the arts to Protestantism; insisted on the practicality of the arts to practical-minded Americans; indicated the uses of the past to present-minded Americans; welcomed the age of internationalism, just when America was leaving its age of provincial development; and, finally, exhibited that the American scholar was up and about his chores and equal to them.

CHAPTER 7

The Open Strings,
Not the Mute, of Fame

JOHN JAY CHAPMAN was a bookman. It had been his destiny to be concerned all his life with books, writers, and the essence of books—ideas vivified in art. The memorial notice which Alexander D. Noyes, secretary of the Century Association, wrote for the annual report of the Century Club for 1934 was impressionistically accurate: "Fellow-Clubmen were apt to meet John Jay Chapman in the library, where the stout and slightly stooping figure, the earnest face, the half-read book tucked under the left arm while the right hand filled a pipe from the deftly-poised tobacco-pouch, will always belong to memories of the place."[1]

John Jay Chapman was a writer—a creature who writes because he has to. His bibliography of printed and unpublished poems, plays, memoirs, addresses, biography, letters to the editor, and essays adds up to several hundred items. His twenty-five books elicited dozens of reviews and notices. Between 1890 and 1930, he published in at least thirty-three different magazines and in half a dozen newspapers here and abroad. His correspondents ran into the hundreds; his letters, into the thousands.

Chapman was also a critic who had to be heard. His pamphlets on Catholicism and against Al Smith were read over radio station WHAP in New York City. He wanted to be read. He published frequently at his own expense. He desired a writer's fame and gained the joy of fulfillment. "You needn't think I am going to die undiscovered. I've been *discovered*, by Jove," he wrote to his mother after receiving his honorary degree at Yale in 1916. A few months later he chortled: "J'ai debuté en France sous le nom supposé de 'James Joe' Chapman le célèbre, etc., appelatifs qui m'ont beaucoup plaît, d'ailleurs." And after the attention he received in the leading article of the London *Times Literary Supplement* of August 14, 1930, he exclaimed: "I'm an international link."[2]

From the distance the anonymous author of the London *Times* essay saw Chapman in a light Chapman himself did not disavow. Chapman was a force, an idealistic American moralist, and a candid and earnest propounder of the difficult but simple axiom that more Christian morality applied to American problems would make them less acute. Chapman was a poet rather than a critic, an enthusiast rather than a scholar, and a quickener of impulsive individualism rather than a temperate expositor who saw much good on both sides of an issue. The English critic apparently saw England less harried by bossism, Mammon, and the timidity of its citizenry than America was in Chapman's eyes; for the Establishment was not yet the target of angry young men. Chapman was pleasant reading but hardly doctrinal for England: "he need not be taken as representing anything; his gifts and his sympathies are delightful in themselves."[3]

The view from this side of the Atlantic, Edmund Wilson's, had a richer appreciation for Chapman's service to the efforts of pioneering domestic political reform although Wilson was nettled by the question of why Chapman had been ineffectual. He concluded that "it is as a prophet and a sage rather than as an agitator that Chapman is to find his destiny."[4] Before Chapman died on November 4, 1933, he knew that he was not only an international link but also an international critical problem.

Apart from the quiet, unpublicized carrying power of Chapman's own words felt by numerous readers who at random have picked up some of his books and have been moved to admiration and thought, Chapman's reputation has been the creation of an identifiable (but not in any sense

organized) group of former friends, pre-eminently Owen
Wister, M. A. DeWolfe Howe, and Edmund Wilson. Chapman
has exerted influence upon a small corps of scholars, teachers,
and writers. Besides, there are at least three doctoral dissertations on Chapman which, considering his scorn for such white-
collar burglars of scholarship, is a sizable irony that Chapman
himself would have relished.

Owen Wister's *Two Appreciations of John Jay Chapman,*
a privately printed collection of a *Yale Review* (1922) book
review of *William Lloyd Garrison* and a reprint of Wister's
memoir of Chapman published in the *Atlantic Monthly* (May,
1934), began the accumulating assessments of Chapman's
achievement. Wister was undeniably correct in locating the
living center of Chapman's thought:

> Throughout his work, prose or verse, runs his message
> to his country, and whether he be talking about municipal
> politics or the Greek genius, the message is always
> religious. . . . Whenever he savagely rips the present
> open, the future is coming, the future is all right. Hope
> lies invariably at the bottom of his Pandora box, hope
> rooted in an impregnable faith. . . . It was not against
> the faith of Rome or against anyone's faith that Chapman
> made his too violent war. He placed faith, no matter how
> formulated, above every good in the world, and loss of
> faith above every other evil.

It is clear from unpublished letters and the *Memoir* that
Wister would have written a first-rate biography of Chapman,
but the family gave the task to M. A. DeWolfe Howe. His
John Jay Chapman and His Letters, which appeared in 1937,
started the cycles of reinterpretation.

Howe had known Chapman for many years. In addition,
Howe knew firsthand the almost vanished milieux of older
literary Boston and New York. By filling half the biography
with Chapman's personality-rich letters, Howe fashioned an
excellent way to introduce Chapman in the late 1930's to an
audience that hardly knew him, that with difficulty re-

membered his times, and that was anxious about depression at home and war abroad. To read the mixed reviews of Howe's book is to understand that Howe's audience had no patience with and no time for what Chapman had to say. Besides, Chapman's full record of writing was not assessed. The biographical record won over the criticism of his ideas.

Howe restrained himself well, considering that Chapman was seriously at odds with the Beacon Street world Howe honored. From a small mountain of papers Howe rescued a biographical picture of an "aristophile . . . catholic and . . . eclectic . . . a religious mystic . . . an individual in revolt . . . a figure of passion, ferocity, and tenderness . . . blundering and arrogant . . . confident often savage . . . a genius . . . a prophet." But Howe, too, felt the human and artistic need to bind the distracting variety of Chapman's life within the tidy boards of a book:

> One thing seems certain—that for all the diversity, or as it was sometimes thought, the perversity, of his manifesta-tion, for all the contradiction between what was best and what was worst in them, a single unifying thread ran through the fabric of his life, the thread of deep, con-tinuous concern for the spiritual realities of human existence, the ultimate truth underlying the relation be-tween the temporal seen and the eternal unseen.
>
> (3)

Howe must be complimented on this score. He did not impose this pattern on Chapman's life; he exposed it.

It is a despair to the man-in-the-street to deal with the unsteady, frequently contradictory, opinions stated by men of taste about a literary matter, book, or person. It is a more constant phenomenon to students of literature. Howe's book set off a cacaphony of criticism. Howe had touched a nerve of opinion. Apparently more people in 1937 remembered Chapman than scant literary allusions to him indicated. Amy Loveman was unimpressed; Zoltan Haraszati could not quite explain why Chapman lost his pertinent usefulness unless it was his diffuseness that handicapped his readers. A friend, Dickinson S. Miller, suggested that Chapman had been spoiled, curiously enough, by not listening seriously to the constructive suggestions of his critics.

Claude M. Fuess admitted to the justness of Chapman's diagnosis of the debilitating American maladies, but he failed to find Chapman handy with remedies. It is perhaps more to the point to say that Chapman did have remedies, but Fuess did not think they were effectual. Who in the 1930's seriously felt that the appeal to private conscience and the avoidance of organizations were the avenues out of social distress? (In the age of "sit-downs" and the Spanish Civil War, who but the betrayed heroes of Dos Passos took those ways out, and what was their fate?) Royal Cortissoz was unwittingly unkind to Chapman when he tried to sum him up in the phrase " a Don Quixote born out of his time." If a phrase must try to do the impossible of summing up Chapman's life and works, Wister's epithet "a belated Abolitionist" is closer to the evasive truth.

Mark Van Doren could wonder at Chapman the letter writer, reformer, and mystic, but Chapman's over-publicized anti-social prejudices had made Chapman act like "any over-heated upperclass savage." To Van Doren the man got in the way of the artist. Ellery Sedgwick was sure Chapman's fame would pass with the death of Chapman's friends. To Sedgwick, Chapman was tied to ephemera of the times; to Howard Mumford Jones, Chapman had "scarcely lived in the current of his time." Chapman's son and literary executor, Chanler A. Chapman, felt compelled to correct Jones: "I have heard him accused of being ill advised, but never before of being a recluse." The pot of reputation boiled, creating much vapor and a little solid residue.

Lucien Price and Kenneth Murdock were decidedly more perceptive of the cohering force that religion had exerted in Chapman's life. They understood, also, the disqualifying part his strongly exclusive middle-class sympathies played in not enlisting reader support either from the many readers of the working class or from the fewer writers and critics who had enlisted in causes of social significance, some of them doctrinaire causes. Particularly helpful in correcting the distortion of personal prejudice, the unfamiliarity of readers with the large body of Chapman's work published sporadically over thirty-four years, and the impatience with Chapman's old-fashioned but irrefutable position of life lived according to moral principle and not profit-making expediency has been the criticism of Edmund Wilson, Jacques Barzun, and, most recently, Richard Hovey.

Wilson's essay "John Jay Chapman: The Mute and the Strings," prompted by Wilson's review of Howe's book, is available in *The Triple Thinkers*. It is still today the best short introduction to the ideas and times of Chapman. In it Wilson asked for a collected edition of Chapman's works, a request as yet unfulfilled. Wilson recognized what he wrote and what he avoided writing about, his letter writing art, and his discovery of the epochal American collaboration of business and government with consequent injury to culture in the United States. Chapman was "the non-socialist political radical," an uncommon American figure, a critic-teacher better than "colonial schoolmasters" More and Babbitt, and an anticipator of the salutary anti-provincial American criticism of H. L. Mencken and Van Wyck Brooks.

Wilson was, however, quite unable to meld the earlier with the later Chapman, the reformer with the Dutchess County, New York, Hudson River squire: "The second half of Chapman's career must inevitably be surprising and depressing, though not entirely disappointing, to one who has been stirred by the first. Though he had been able to throw away his crutches, he was to remain, in a deeper sense, a crippled man all the rest of his life."[5]

Muriel Rukeyser in *A Turning Wind* (1939) saw him as "a charred man, reborn too often," a victim of his religious nature. Ever since Wilson's essay, critics like Stocking and Hovey have successfully put the halves—if, indeed, they were halves—together to try to understand the mysterious energy of the man, to try to contain the achievement of the man. But it was Wilson's inclusion of the Emerson essay in *The Shock of Recognition* (1943) that recalled Chapman to the attention of thousands of teachers and students of American literature.

Jacques Barzun in 1947 did not see either a crippled man or a charred man in Chapman; he saw on him a label in capitals: JOHN JAY CHAPMAN: CRITIC FIRST CLASS; then perhaps in smaller type, as a footnote: *"Philosophical writer, sociologist, humorist."* Not to have discerned this, Barzun pointed out, revealed a deep fault in American thought. We were deficient in the habit of reading cultural critics of the stature of De Tocqueville, Whitman, and Chapman—writers who wrote against the grain of American life. Linked in subject matter to the tradition of western Europe, Chapman applied his American moralism to a scrutiny of the past and the present to better the future, especially through the agency of education. Idiosyncrasy aside, and his humor understood, beneath all that he wrote was Chapman's optimistic thesis that "intellect can be a social force," a particularly pertinent suggestion (in 1947) in a post-war inflation period when television was making aggressive strides in its capture of the air around us. Barzun's essay in the February, 1947, *Atlantic Monthly* became the nucleus of an expanded prefatory essay to *The Selected Writings of John Jay Chapman* in 1957. This edition was unfortunately quite removed from the collected works called for by Wilson twenty years earlier.

What writings represent Chapman steadily and whole is questionable, but it is futile to quarrel with an anthologist's choice, for it is his option to tell the time by his own watch. Barzun's anthology served its purpose in offering Chapman to a reading public who could no longer plead ignorance of his writing. In a measure, it helped to prepare the market for the latest critical study, Richard Hovey's *John Jay Chapman . . . An American Mind* (1959).

Hovey's book, a "mental biography," resorted to psychoanalytical hypotheses to explain the crucial and perplexingly neurotic incidents of Chapman's life. Chapman's behavior was at times puzzling, and Hovey makes it convincingly clear that, whatever guilt feelings drove him to his remorseful acts, Chapman the artist did not write his criticism under the influence of his sporadic nervous strains. Hovey supplied new details that itemized both Chapman's private agony and his public behavior. He fell into the ineluctable Chapman trap: he quoted generously from Chapman's writings. Chapman is inescapably quotable—a joyous embarrassment to all who write about him. Hovey supplemented the interpretation of Howe, adjusted that of Wilson, and completed that of Barzun.

That all of Hovey's chapters are named in biblical quotations is fair to Chapman. The reader who does not approach Chapman with the acceptance of his religiousness does injustice to himself and to Chapman who candidly asked to be read in this fashion. This fact illuminates the relationship Chapman established with Emerson, and it also distinctly marks the difference between the two men.

It is critically insufficient to call Chapman a reborn Emerson. He was Emerson with a difference. The two men criticized the same things. The two men were sharply intuitive, richly associative, and sympathetically ethical in their demands for the perfection of the individual and, by extension, of society. But—and it is a crucial but—where Emerson had edited the familiar God from his essays, his poems, and his Transcendentalism, Chapman the redactor of the American past had written God back into the documents, the history, the dreams and the nightmares, and the promises of American life. Chapman's American scholar was different from Emerson's. Chapman's scholar was urged to study not nature capitalized but God. Taking a cue from Emerson's Divinity School Address, which supplemented the prescription for the success of the American scholar, Chapman could have pointed to his warrant: "It is the office of a true preacher," Emerson had told the senior class of the Harvard

Divinity School that summer evening in 1838, "to show us that God is, not was; that He speaketh, not spake."

The critical American reading public of Chapman's lifetime (and also the audience of Howe's biography) could and did balk at treating the world's new problems by recourse to the old solution. It must be conceded that Chapman among our secular writers had more intimations of on-coming religious revivals than any non-professional revivalist ever had, more certainly than any other American writer shows. Hardly does the reader get involved in an intellectual journey exploring a set of facts with Chapman than he is switched to the Celestial Railroad. True, it was an independently owned, privately run, customer-sharing-the-profits-run railroad; but it was, just the same, an express to heaven. The mood of Chapman's audience was to adopt other (in Chapman's view, misleading) approaches—strikes, unions, science, social science, or psychology. The American temper of Chapman's readers had a strong touch of Huck Finn's skepticism of having been "there" before.

In addition, Chapman's refusal (like Emerson's) to join and work with organizations, and Chapman's mysticism (like Emerson's) alienated the organization-mindedness and the preference for pragmatism and expediency of twentieth-century American thinking. When Chapman pleaded for Emerson's nineteenth-century self-reliant man to be reborn in the twentieth century as the big individual, his readers read but could not believe in his rebirth. The Goliaths of big war, big business, big wealth, big corruption, big unions, big poverty, big malnutrition, big unemployment, big armies, big science, big technology, and big bombs—all these overmatched, plainly and tragically, the Davidic individual. Yet Chapman's optimism was for David, who was, let us note, also an artist, a singer of Psalms to the Lord God. The American public in the twentieth century accelerates in everything including its secularization of values. It reads Chapman (if it reads him at all) understanding that he stood for nothing it stands for, and reads him understanding that he stood for something long ago abandoned—the old American dream abandoned for an empirical, un-utopian modernism.

With these reasons in mind, we can understand why the acute, sensitive, and sensible Alfred Kazin—richly aware of both the high seas and the deep currents running in American life—recently and erroneously bestowed on Chapman the epithet of our times. With distaste associated with the adjective, Kazin called Chapman "a leftover Transcendentalist."[6] Each age writes its own books, rewrites history, composes its obituaries, shapes its dreams, draws up its menu, and, understandably, disdains leftovers. When Owen Wister called Chapman "a belated Abolitionist" and when Kazin calls Chapman "a leftover Transcendentalist," we have offered to us two major views of the American past that qualify our present. The abolitionist intent of Chapman—to eliminate the masks of intellectual and social habits of slavery, political timidity, and the happy family adjustment to things as they are—is the more accurate definition of Chapman's concern with American life. Behind the American masks were a stultifying commercialism, an insipid conventional culture, and a potential mob cruelty nauseously kinetic in Coatesville, Pennsylvania, in 1911 and in Oxford, Mississippi, in 1962. Recently reporting his travels in the United States in *Travels with Charley* (1962), John Steinbeck recorded that Chapman's indictment against society in America still stands and that his three major grievances need redress.

Religion, then, "green-growing religion" was Chapman's *donnée*. Criticism acknowledges this and goes on from there. Religion nourished by a mystic's confidence in intuition supplied Chapman with the sense of time past, present, and future. Disguised frequently, it gave him the energy to improve, agitate, lash, love, press, abide, and make prophecies. It also comprehended all the fractional parts of the universe men wrote ponderously about, thought scientifically of, hoped educationally for, and strained to express in delicious music.

The mention of music brings up one more recurrent matter in the Chapman literature. There is a curious repetition in the biography by Howe, the appreciation by Wister, the critical essay by Wilson, and the latest biography by Hovey. All end by quoting the same incident—his last words to his wife.

For almost a week after Chapman had been operated on in the Vassar Hospital in Poughkeepsie, New York, he lingered in pain. Semiconscious from sedatives and just before he died, he said to his wife, plucking her fingers, "I want to take it away, I want to take it away!"

" 'What?' I asked, 'the pillow?' "

"No," he said, "the mute, the mute. I want to play on the open strings."

Last words of sinners and saints are symbolically precious. In Chapman's case, because he was almost always so cleanly articulate, it is understandable that those who have studied patiently to understand him are provoked and teased by the symbolic intent of the distinction between the mute and the open strings. What joy or failure in music or speech, in being or doing, or in wanting or having, in willing or accepting lies behind the hieroglyphic of his image is impossible to say with surety.

Music had been in its intensest moments "a deification" to Chapman. He had struggled with words all his life. Acutely sensitive to music, to the effort of words, to the writer's envy for the illusory ease of the effortless, wordless artist of another medium—painter or sculptor or, especially, musician—Chapman aspired romantically and mystically to the highest expression: the most unambiguous, the clearest expression; the unmuted, open-stringed expression of his understanding. All his life he had nourished a reverence for the *maestro* in music. Criticism, he had insisted, was impotent against Bach's fugues, Beethoven's progressions, and Mendelssohn's melodies.

In the hierarchy of things available to man, according to the Book of Common Prayer in Chapman's Episcopal Church worship, "in returning and rest . . . in quietness and in confidence," in silence man knew God. Next to the paradoxical silence that seems difficult to associate with John Jay Chapman, music was to him the music that to Dante "draws the soul most in desire." Music stirred Chapman's heart in hiding even as the Windhover had stirred Gerard Manley Hopkins' heart to praise of God. Hopkins wrote, and dedicated the poem to Christ: "My heart in hiding/Stirred for a bird,—the achieve of, the mastery of the thing!" So Chapman felt about music, a *logos* of the mystic and enthusiast. It was at one with Dante's "love that moves the sun and the other stars."

It is tempting to pin Chapman's achievement to a phrase, but his variety defeats the attempt. Little influences sometimes too easily deflected, but not for long, the force he gathered and spent upon the world. The torque of the times he lived in twisted him, too. Some critics would hold his diffuseness against him and label it quixotism. To be himself, he could not have been anything but an anti-specialist. If he was a Don Quixote, Chapman gives us back Yeats's image of a world without zest in which "The best lack all conviction, while the worst/Are full of passionate intensity"—and so in the end we esteem him for renewing our faltering humanity.

Chapman reminds American readers of what they have been and might be. In him and his family, history itself is caught up and held. His writings reveal the heritage of major ideas that tumble in almost disorderly haste through the brief and intense course of American history—despite the attempts of a Max Lerner, Van Wyck Brooks, Wilson, or Kazin to get them to march in ranks and series.

The Huguenot Jay and Puritan Chapman families brought to America a vision bound in their family Bibles. Both families infused their primitive Protestant piety into the beginnings of what was to be a Christian commonwealth. Shared by John Jay, Enlightenment optimism established the American state. Libertarian romanticism, shared by later Jays and Chapmans in their Abolitionism, opposed the clogging conservatisms of law, property, and the cash nexus which compromised American idealism. Business rebuked, reformed, and also invigorated by the Civil War became the neuter ground on which disunited American energies became reconciled. Chapman's father was connected with the Wall Street of the Gilded Age; but, reared in the Gilded Age, John Jay Chapman never for one moment confused it with America's Golden Age that could come if—. At this point John Jay Chapman's writings continued the idealisms of the Puritan Settlement, the Revolutionary War, the Enlightenment secularism, Romantic individualism, and Transcendental moralism and estheticism; to these he added practical political reform and broad cultural criticism. The family ideals of excellence and virtue, of individual education and public service, of private integrity and strenuous citizenship—all accumulated and combined in John Jay Chapman. Family history starting in the Europe of the seventeenth century burgeoned into accomplishment in America, persisting well into the twentieth century. To follow the chronicle of the two families is to study in concentration the history of America. Chapman augmented the chronicle by becoming the only belletrist among them.

Chapman's fame is sounded with a mute by some, on the open strings by others. His causes were linked with the decline of influence in American life of his upper middle class, a decline recorded in the gas-light fiction of James, Howells, and Wharton. He upbraided his class for neglect of responsibility for leadership. The fault was not in not knowing but in not doing. Error was the defect, not ignorance. The fact is that the power of "the four hundred," once a power élite in early America, was disappearing into what is today almost 200,000,000 people. Along with the disappearing élite went the power of the nineteenth-century essay and essayist to move millions; in its stead, came the mass media. Chapman was a nineteenth-century gentleman, and gentlemen were going out of fashion not only in Boston and New York but also in Washington, D.C., Chicago, San Francisco, and Dallas. His valuable conservationism is too easily confused with a conservatism for which the discriminating popular ballot in America shows no electoral enthusiasm.

Often he made palpable hits on American targets worth destroying. His concern for quality education in a quantity-minded America cannot be brushed aside as irrelevant to us. Too often the reader seeking a program is rewarded only by a feeling of enthusiasm to do something—but *what* and *how* are not precisely clear. Understandably, he feels disappointed. The amorphous condition of American education today is an extension of a condition Chapman saw being created in America. Our struggle today to define a general and a liberal education in terms of a college curriculum is the consequence of yesterday's cause: the neglect of humanistic education in a get-up-and-go American civilization. It may be our error that today the problems seem new; but in many cases they are new only in their gigantism. When a wall is erected in Berlin, type in newspapers all over the world—even in emerging Africa—wobbles in excitement. We react mindlessly, recklessly, and hysterically—as if there had never before been walls built in history. F. Scott Fitzgerald was concerned that there were no second acts in America. Chapman reminds us that we are ignorant of prologues to the first act.

The open-stringed music Chapman wanted to make even to the last words of his energetic life symbolizes the man of this world who refuses in his virility to take life without thought, without protest, without the cry or the laugh, and without the word or the music that are the marks of his humanity.

Chapman relished throwing the stone of the next world at this one. But it does not sum him up. Consider this from "The Indian Saint" contained in *Letters and Religion*: "The mysticisms of the East begin with a higher symbolism and seem never to reach an application. I am not sure that I have intellect enough to follow your doctrine, says the Christian to the Hindu, to the Buddhist, to the Taoist. What is the bearing of your thought upon the position of women in the East?" Chapman could not sacrifice human dignity, not even to a religious system. He enjoyed, too, throwing a real stone from this world at the next.

Notes and References

Chapter Two

1. *John Jay Chapman and His Letters* (Boston, 1937), p. 32. (Subsequently referred to as Howe.)
2. Chapman, *Retrospections*, Howe, p. 49.
3. An incident like this turns up in William C. Bullitt's novel, *It's Not Done* (New York, 1926), which in addition reflects the sinking of the patrician class in America by the parvenu tycoons of the Gilded Age. The novel reflects the changes forced upon Main Line values 1880-1925.
4. Howe, p. 66.
5. *Ibid.*, p. 69.

Chapter Three

1. See Ralph Thompson, *American Literary Annuals and Gift Books, 1825-65* (New York, 1936).
2. Chapman, *Causes and Consequences* (New York, 1898), pp. 154-55.
3. *Ibid.*, p. 75.
4. *Ibid.*, p. 121.
5. Chapman, *Practical Agitation* (New York, 1900), p. 14.
6. *Ibid.*, p. 52.
7. *Ibid.*, p. 143.
8. *Annals of the Academy of American Political and Social Science*, XII (July, 1898), 15.
9. *Nation*, LXX (May 31, 1900), 247.
10. Chapman, *The Maid's Forgiveness* (New York, 1908), p. 86.
11. Chapman, *Memories and Milestones* (New York, 1915), pp. 225-32.
12. Chapman, *Songs and Poems* (New York, 1919), p. 67.
13. Quoted Howe, p. 341.
14. David Stocking in his University of Michigan doctoral dissertation, "The Ideas of John Jay Chapman" (1949), ably and understandingly records the philosophic assumptions of Chapman's political activity and illuminates his shift from politics to education.
15. *Commonweal*, I (December 10, 1924), 116.
16. See Chapter X, pp. 285-86, of Richard Hovey's recent and compassionate biography, *John Jay Chapman* (New York, 1959), for a fuller picture of Chapman's state of mind then, and the sonnet. One note more: every so often this anti-Semitic moment in Chapman's life stirs up anger in critics. These critics are urged

to read Chapman's "Memoir of Isaac H. Klein" read at a memorial service to Klein on January 11, 1920. Isaac H. Klein (1861-1919) was Jewish; he was Chapman's mentor in metropolitan politics; he worked with Chapman in the Good Government Clubs; Klein's office was the editorial office of the *Political Nursery*. The memoir is in the files of the *Madison House News*, a journal of the Madison House, which was a youth settlement house in New York City. Late in his life, Klein turned from practical political reform activities to practical youth settlement work. He was an active trustee of Madison House.

Chapter Four

1. *The Two Philosophers* (Boston, 1892), p. 37.
2. *Retrospections*, Howe, p. 194.
3. *New Horizons in American Life* (New York, 1932), p. 31.
4. Chapman printed the address, "The Unity of Human Nature," in the *Nursery* and collected it in *Learning and Other Essays* (New York, 1910), pp. 175-90.
5. *New Horizons*, pp. 40-41, 46.
6. *Ibid.*, p. 47-48.
7. Chapman collected this essay in *Memories and Milestones*, pp. 129-45.
8. *Science*, XXX (October 1, 1909), 441.
9. *Learning and Other Essays*, p. 29.
10. *Memories and Milestones*, pp. 249-50.
11. "The New Dawn in Education," *Forum*, LXXV (April, 1926), 608; an uncollected essay. Irresponsibility in education matched American financial exuberance in the Twenties: "Today we in America are passing through an access, a tornado, a frenzy of prosperity."
12. "Irreducible Elements in the Melting Pot," *Yale Review*, XV (N. S.) (April, 1926), 582-84; an uncollected book review of Gino Speranza's *Race or Nation* (New York, 1925).
13. *Letters and Religion*, p. 4.
14. Howe, pp. 170-71.
15. *Letters and Religion*, pp. 44-45.
16. Porter Sargent, *A Handbook of Private Schools for American Boys and Girls*, 31st ed. (Boston, 1948), p. 50.

Chapter Five

1. See Howe, pp. 73, 100, 454.
2. *Ibid.*, p. 33.
3. *Ibid.*, p. 83.

4. *Ibid.*, pp. 129-30.
5. *Ibid.*, pp. 418, 200, 410.
6. *Ibid.*, pp. 200-2.
7. Chapman, "On Faith," *Nursery*, III (July, 1899), 4.
8. Chapman, *Learning and Other Essays*, pp. 194-95.
9. Chapman, "Luxury," *Nursery*, IV (April, 1900), 3-4.
10. *Notes on Religion*, pp. 43-44.
11. George Santayana, "The Alleged Catholic Danger," *New Republic*, V (January 15, 1916), 269-71.
12. "Mr. Chapman Replies to Mr. Cram," *Commonweal*, I (December 10, 1924), 116.
13. Chapman, "Strike at the Source," *Forum*, LXXIII (April, 1925), 449-57. Chapman did not collect this essay, but he did print it privately and distributed it.
14. Edmund Wilson, *The Triple Thinkers* (New York, 1948), p. 161. For background details, interested readers are directed to John Higham, *Strangers in the Land* (New York, 1963).
15. Chapman, *Letters and Religion*, p. 35.
16. Emerson wrote in "Nominalist and Realist": "Nature will not remain orbed in thought, but rushes into persons."
17. Chapman, *Letters and Religion*, p. 64.
18. *Ibid.*, p. 52.

Chapter Six

1. Howe, p. 120.
2. *Ibid.*, p. 125.
3. *Ibid.*, pp. 150, 76.
4. *Emerson and Other Essays* (New York, 1898), pp. 107-8.
5. *Ibid.*, p. 78.
6. Henry Grafton Chapman, "Some Aspects of American Barbarism," *Bachelor of Arts*, II (February, 1896), 772.
7. Max Nordau, *Degeneration*, 9th ed. (New York, 1897), p. 550. See pp. 230-32 for Nordau on Whitman.
8. *Emerson and Other Essays*, pp. 111-28.
9. *William Lloyd Garrison* (New York, 1921), p. 265.
10. See Leon Edel (ed.), *Henry James, The American Essays* (New York, 1956), pp. 240-41.
11. Chapman, "Robert Browning," *Emerson and Other Essays*, p. 187.
12. *Ibid.*, "Kipling," *Nursery*, II (April, 1899), 8-10.
13. *Ibid.*, "Robert Louis Stevenson," *Emerson and Other Essays*, pp. 217-47.
14. *Ibid.*, *Greek Genius* (New York, 1915), p. 15.
15. *Ibid.*, "Shakespeare," *Greek Genius*, p. 173.

16. *Ibid., A Glance Toward Shakespeare* (Boston, 1925), p. 116.

17. *Ibid.,* "A Study of Romeo," *Emerson and Other Essays,* p. 149.

18. *Ibid.,* "Balzac," *Greek Genius,* pp. 227, 248, 249.

19. *Emerson and Other Essays,* p. 170.

20. See G. A. Borgese, "On Dante Criticism," *Annual Reports of the Dante Society* (Cambridge, Mass., 1936), pp. 19-70.

21. Angelina La Piana, *Dante's American Pilgrimage* (New Haven, 1948), pp. 182ff.

22. Chapman, *Letters and Religion,* p. 35.

Chapter Seven

1. *Reports, Constitution, By-Laws and List of Members of The Century Association for the Year 1934* (No publisher), p. 53. At the Century Club where Chapman spent much time he could meet, among others, the following members: Nicholas Murray Butler, Walter Damrosch, John Dewey, Learned Hand, M. A. DeWolfe Howe, Walter Lippmann, F. D. Roosevelt, Thornton Wilder, and Edmund Wilson.

2. Howe, pp. 320, 326, 442.

3. "An American Moralist," The (London) *Times Literary Supplement,* August 14, 1930, p. 646.

4. Edmund Wilson, "John Jay Chapman," *New Republic,* LIX (May 22, 1929), 28-33.

5. Edmund Wilson, *The Triple Thinkers* (New York, 1948), p. 149.

6. Alfred Kazin, *Contemporaries* (Boston, 1962), p. 64.

Selected Bibliography

PRIMARY SOURCES

A. *Chapman's Chief Works*

The Two Philosophers: A Quaint and Sad Comedy. Boston: J. G. Cupples, 1892.

Emerson and Other Essays. New York: Charles Scribner's Sons, 1898. Republished, New York: Moffat, Yard & Co., 1909.

Causes and Consequences. New York: Charles Scribner's Sons, 1898. Republished, New York: Moffat, Yard & Co., 1909.

Practical Agitation. New York: Charles Scribner's Sons, 1898. Republished, New York: Moffat, Yard & Co., 1909.

Four Plays for Children. New York: Moffat, Yard & Co., 1908.

The Maid's Forgiveness: A Play. New York: Moffat, Yard & Co., 1908.

A Sausage from Bologna: A Comedy in Four Acts. New York: Moffat, Yard & Co., 1909.

Learning and Other Essays. New York: Moffat, Yard & Co., 1910.

The Treason and Death of Benedict Arnold: A Play for a Greek Theatre. New York: Moffat, Yard & Co., 1910.

Neptune's Isle and Other Plays for Children. New York: Moffat, Yard & Co., 1911.

William Lloyd Garrison. New York: Moffat, Yard & Co., 1913. Republished, with added materials, Boston: Atlantic Monthly Press, 1921.

Deutschland über Alles; or, Germany Speaks. New York: G. P. Putnam's Sons, 1914.

Homeric Scenes: Hector's Farewell and The Wrath of Achilles. New York: Laurence J. Gomme, 1914.

Greek Genius and Other Essays. New York: Moffat, Yard & Co., 1915.

Memories and Milestones. New York: Moffat, Yard & Co., 1915.

Notes on Religion. New York: Laurence J. Gomme, 1915. Second edition, 1916; reprinted 1922.

Washington et Lafayette. [Traduit par Émile Legouis.] Paris: Imprimerie Chaix, 1915.

Cupid and Psyche. New York: Laurence J. Gomme, 1916.

Victor Chapman's Letters from France, with a Memoir by John Jay Chapman. New York: Macmillan Co., 1917.

Songs and Poems. New York: Charles Scribner's Sons, 1919.

A Glance Toward Shakespeare. Boston: Atlantic Monthly Press, 1922.

Letters and Religion. Boston: Atlantic Monthly Press, 1924.

Dante. Boston: Houghton Mifflin Co., 1927.

Two Greek Plays: The Philoctetes of Sophocles and the Medea of Euripides—Done into English. Boston: Houghton Mifflin Co., 1928.

The Antigone of Sophocles. Boston: Houghton Mifflin Co., 1929.

Lucian, Plato and Greek Morals. Boston: Houghton Mifflin Co., 1931.

New Horizons in American Life. New York: Columbia University Press, 1932.

B. *Chapman's Uncollected Works*

Note: There are close to one hundred uncollected Chapman items. There are unpublished letters and manuscripts in the Houghton Library, Harvard University. The selected list below supplies the basic data of this interpretation. The chronological listing indicates the persistence and productivity of Chapman, the variety of his thought, and the variety of audiences he reached.

The Political Nursery, a periodical, New York, March, 1897-January, 1901. Bound volumes are available in the libraries of Columbia, Cornell, Harvard, Princeton, and Yale universities; the New York Public Library at 42nd Street, New York, and the Library of the State of New York at Albany.

"The Harvard Classics and Harvard." *Science,* XXX New Series (October 1, 1909), 440-43.

"John Bigelow." *American Magazine,* LXIX (February, 1910), 454-57.

"The Passing of a Great Bogey." *Vanity Fair,* X (October, 1918), 65.

"Lincoln and Hamlet." *North American Review,* CCIX (March, 1919), 371-79.

"Art in Our Universities." *Vanity Fair,* XII (April, 1919), 29, 90, 92.

"Harvard's Plight." *Vanity Fair,* XII (May, 1919), 30, 84.

"A New Menace to Education." *Vanity Fair,* XII (June, 1919), 27, 88.

"Portrait of Josiah Royce, the Philosopher." *Outlook,* CXXII (July 2, 1919), 322-27.

"McKim, Mead and White." *Vanity Fair,* XIII (September, 1919), 27, 102, 104.

"Henry Ford's Place in History." *Vanity Fair,* XII (December, 1919), 51.

"Imaginary Obituaries: E. S. Martin." *Vanity Fair*, XIII (January, 1920), 55.

"Memoir of Isaac H. Klein." *Madison House News*, January, 1920.

"Imaginary Obituaries: Percy Stickney Grant." *Vanity Fair*, XIV (March, 1920), 43.

"Imaginary Obituaries: Major George Haven Putnam." *Vanity Fair*, XIV (May, 1920), 73-104.

"Highbrows, Guttersnipes and Taxpayers." *Vanity Fair*, XIV (June, 1920), 47, 116.

"American Universities and the Post-Victorian Age." *Princeton Alumni Weekly*, XXIII (April 18, 1923), 581-83.

"Concerning Our Slovenly English." New York *Times Book Review*, May 13, 1923, p. 2.

"Concerning Our Slovenly Thinking." New York *Times Book Review*, June 10, 1923, p. 4.

"Drink and the Tyranny of Dogma." *Outlook*, CXXXVI (January 16, 1924), 107-9.

"Why Not Speak Out?" *Independent*, CXIII (August 16, 1924), 91-92.

"Harvard and Business." *Harvard Graduates' Magazine*, XXXIII (September, 1924), 37-45.

"Our Universities." *School and Society*, XX (September 20, 1924), 365-68.

"In Memory of Edgar Allan Poe." New York *Times Book Review*, November 2, 1924, p. 2.

"Our Great Private Schools." *Atlantic Monthly*, CXXXIV (December, 1924), 742-44.

"Strike at the Source." *Forum*, LXXIII (April, 1925), 449-57.

"America's Fear Complex." *Forum*, LXXV (May, 1926), 734-37.

"Osborne's Place in Historic Criminology." *Harvard Graduates' Magazine*, XXV (June, 1927), 599-605.

"The Roman Catholic Mind: Extract from My Secret Journal." Distributed by Radio Station WHAP, New York City, 1920.

"Antigone and Prohibition." *New Republic*, LX (September 11, 1929), 92-95.

"Retrospections," unpublished autobiography [1931?].

"Goethe," unpublished manuscript [1932?].

Uncollected poetry, 1920-29, published in the *Atlantic Monthly, Century, Forum, Harper's Magazine, Harvard Graduates' Magazine*, New York *Herald Tribune Books, Independent, Sewanee Review, Scribner's* and *Yale Review*.

Eight uncollected book reviews in the *Yale Review*: April, July, October 1926; July 1927; January, April 1928; December 1930; and March 1931.

SECONDARY SOURCES

A. *Bibliography*

There is no complete and reliable bibliography of Chapman's work. Interested readers are directed to the bibliographies appended to the doctoral dissertations of Bernstein, Hovey, and Stocking, and to Hovey's biography (below).

B. *Doctoral Dissertations*

BERNSTEIN, MELVIN H. "The Mind of John Jay Chapman." New York University, 1951. Chapman's various published works are organically related to his inheritance, his biography, and his times.

HOVEY, RICHARD B. "John Jay Chapman: The Early Years." Harvard University, 1950. Detailed analysis of the biographical and intellectual origins of Chapman's work through the *Political Nursery.*

STOCKING, DAVID. "The Ideas of John Jay Chapman." University of Michigan, 1950. Traces the turning of Chapman's early individualism and skepticism into his later quietism and humanism; but Chapman was not a quietist.

C. *Biography*

HOVEY, RICHARD B. *John Jay Chapman . . . An American Mind.* New York: Columbia University Press, 1959. Detailed combination of biography and cultural criticism, leaning heavily on speculation about Chapman's frame of mind that dictated his interests.

HOWE, M. A. DEWOLFE. *John Jay Chapman and His Letters.* Boston: Houghton Mifflin Company, 1937. Best source for the delightful and witty letters of, perhaps, the best letter writer in American literature.

WISTER, OWEN. *Two Appreciations of John Jay Chapman.* New York: Marchbanks Press, 1934. An understanding estimate of a lifelong friend.

D. *Critical and Interpretive*

Anonymous. "A Literary Lawyer," *Munsey's Magazine,* XIX (August, 1898), 797-98. A brief, contemporary notice of praise for the promise of Chapman's literary criticism.

Anonymous. "An American Moralist," London *Times Literary Supplement,* No. 1489 (August 14, 1930), 645-66. The

English critic relished his "against-the-grain" Emersonianism; but complained that his idealism was naively American.

BARZUN, JACQUES (ed.). *The Selected Writings of John Jay Chapman*. New York: Farrar, Straus & Cudahy, 1957. Barzun's "Introduction" is an expanded version of his earlier essay, "Against the Grain: John Jay Chapman," *Atlantic Monthly*, CLXXIX (February, 1947), 120-24. Reading Chapman today would inspire us to redecorate the shabby American house of intellect.

BERNSTEIN, MELVIN H. "John Jay Chapman and the Insurgent Individual," in Harvey Goldberg (ed.), *American Radicals: Some Problems and Personalities*. New York: Monthly Review Press, 1957. Chapman's buoyant protests anticipated the muckrakers of the early 1900's.

BROWN, STUART GERRY. "John Jay Chapman and the Emersonian Gospel," *New England Quarterly*, XXXV (June, 1952), 147-80. Chapman's Emersonianism was a pragmatic idea pertinent to the American climate of opinion in the 1950's.

JAMES, HENRY. *The American Essays*, edited by Leon Edel. New York: Vintage Books, 1956. Paperbound. Chapman's essay on Emerson was in 1898 "the most effective critical attempt made in the United States" to understand Emerson.

SEDGWICK, ELLERY (ed.). *Atlantic Harvest*. Boston: Little, Brown and Co., 1947. Chapman's achievements were not equal to his talents.

STOCKING, DAVID. "John Jay Chapman and Political Reform," *American Quarterly*, II (Spring, 1950), 62-70. Stocking makes a dubious case for Chapman's political failure leading him to mysticism.

WILSON, EDMUND. "John Jay Chapman," *New Republic*, LIX (May 22, 1929), 28-33. This was the first substantial analysis of Chapman's significance, his relation to the American tradition, and a still unheeded plea to reprint his works.

WILSON, EDMUND. *The Triple Thinkers*. New York: Harcourt, Brace, 1938. Reprinted and revised, New York: Oxford University Press, 1948. A collected book review, Wilson's essay established the guide lines of the subsequent scholarly investigation of Chapman.

Index